S0-BRP-822

Shinto

Shinto
The Way Home
THOMAS P. KASULIS

Dimensions of Asian Spirituality

UNIVERSITY OF HAWAI'I PRESS

Honolulu

DIMENSIONS OF ASIAN SPIRITUALITY
Henry Rosemont, Jr., General Editor

This series makes available short but comprehensive works on specific Asian philosophical and religious schools of thought, works focused on a specific region, and works devoted to the full articulation of a concept central to one or more of Asia's spiritual traditions. Series volumes are written by distinguished scholars in the field who not only present their subject in historical context for the nonspecialist reader but also express their own views of the contemporary spiritual relevance of the subject for global citizens of the twenty-first century.

© 2004 University of Hawai'i Press
All rights reserved
Printed in the United States of America
14 13 12 11 10 09   9 8 7 6 5 4

Library of Congress Cataloging-in-Publication Data

Kasulis, Thomas P.
Shinto : the way home / Thomas P. Kasulis.
p. cm.—(Dimensions of Asian spirituality)
Includes bibliographical references and index.
ISBN 0-8248-2794-5 (hardcover : alk. paper)—
ISBN 978-0-8248-2850-9 (pbk. : alk. paper)
1. Shinto. I. Title. II. Series.
BL2220.K38 2004
299.5'61—dc22
2004001297

University of Hawai'i Press books are printed on acid-free paper and meet the guidelines for permanence and durability of the Council on Library Resources.

Designed by Rich Hendel

Printed by The Maple-Vail Book Manufacturing Group

FOR ELLEN

Contents

Editor's Preface

ABOUT THIS SERIES

The University of Hawai'i Press has long been noted for its scholarly publications in and commitment to the field of Asian studies. This series, "Dimensions of Asian Spirituality," is in keeping with that commitment. It is a most appropriate time for such a series to appear. A number of the world's religions—major and minor—originated in Asia, continue to influence the lives of a third of the world's peoples, and should now be seen as global in scope, reach, and impact, with rich and varied resources for every citizen of the twenty-first century to explore.

Religion is at the heart of every culture. To be sure, the members of every culture have also been influenced by climate, geology, and the consequent patterns of economic activity they have developed for the production and distribution of goods. Only a rudimentary knowledge of physical geography is necessary to understand why African sculptors largely employed wood as their medium whereas their Italian Renaissance counterparts worked with marble. But while necessary for understanding cultures—not least our own—matters of geography and economics will not be sufficient: marble is found in China, too, yet the Chinese sculptor carved a bodhisattva, not a pietà, from his block.

In the same way, a mosque, synagogue, cathedral, stupa, and pagoda may be equally beautiful, but they are beautiful in different ways, and the differences cannot be accounted for merely on the basis of the materials used in their construction. Their beauty, their power to inspire awe and invite contemplation, rest largely on the religious view of the world—and the place of human beings in that world—expressed in their architecture. The spiritual dimensions of a culture are reflected significantly not only in art and architecture but in music, myths, poetry, rituals, customs, and patterns of social behavior as well. Therefore it follows that if we wish to understand why and how members of other cultures live as they do, we must understand the religious beliefs and practices to which they adhere.

In the first instance, such understanding of the "other" leads to tolerance, which is surely a good thing. Much of the pain and suffering in the world today is attributable to intolerance, a fear and hatred of those who look, think, and act differently. But as technological changes in communication, production, and transportation shrink the world, more and more people must confront the fact of human diversity in multiple forms—both between and within nations—and hence there is a growing need to advance beyond mere tolerance of difference to an appreciation and even celebration of it.

The evils attendant on intolerance notwithstanding, tolerance alone cannot contribute substantively to making the world a better—and sustainable—place for human beings to live. Mere tolerance is easy for us: I can fully respect your right to believe and worship as you wish, associate with whomever, and say what you will, simply by ignoring you. You assuredly have a right to speak, but not to make me listen.

Yet for most of us who live in economically developed societies, or are among the affluent in developing nations, tolerance is not enough. Ignoring the poverty, disease, and gross inequalities that afflict fully a third of the human race will only exacerbate, not alleviate, the conditions responsible for the misery that generates the violence becoming ever more commonplace throughout the world today. That violence will cease only when the more fortunate among the peoples of the world become active, take up the plight of the less fortunate, and resolve to create a more just world, a resolve that requires a full appreciation of everyone's co-humanity, significant differences in religious beliefs and practices notwithstanding.

Such appreciation should not, of course, oblige everyone to endorse all of the beliefs and practices within their own faith. A growing number of Catholics, for instance, support changes in church practice: a married clergy, the ordination of women, recognition of rights for gays and lesbians, and full reproductive rights for women. Yet they remain Catholics, believing that the tenets of their faith have the conceptual resources to bring about and justify these changes. In the same way, we can also believe—as a number of Muslim women do—that the Qur'an and other Islamic theological writings contain the conceptual resources to overcome the inferior status of women in some Muslim countries. And indeed we can believe that every spiritual tradition has within it the resources to counter older practices inimical to the full flourishing of all the faithful—including the faithful of other traditions as well.

Another reason to advance beyond mere tolerance to appreciation and celebration of the many and varied forms of spiritual expression is virtually a truism: the more we look through the window of another culture's beliefs and practices, the more it becomes a mirror of our own (even for those who follow no religious tradition). We must look carefully and charitably, however, or the reflections become distorted. When studying other religions, most people are inclined to focus on cosmological and ontological questions: What do these people believe about the origin of the world and where it is heading? Do they believe in ghosts? Immortal souls? A creator god?

Answering such metaphysical questions is of course necessary for understanding and appreciating the specific forms and content of the art, music, architecture, rituals, and traditions inspired by the specific religion under study. But the sensitive—and sensible—student will bracket the further question of whether the metaphysical pronouncements are literally true—we must attend carefully to the metaphysics (and theologies) of the religions we study, but questions of their literal truth should be set aside in order to concentrate on a different question: How could a thoughtful, thoroughly decent human being subscribe to such beliefs and attendant practices?

Studied in this light, we may come to appreciate how each religious tradition provides a coherent account of a world not fully amenable to human manipulation or, perhaps, even to full human understanding. The metaphysical pronouncements of the world's religions of course differ measurably from faith to faith, and each has had a significant influence on the physical expressions of the respective faith in synagogues, stupas, mosques, pagodas, and cathedrals. Despite these differences between the buildings, however, the careful and sensitive observer can see the spiritual dimensions of human life that these sacred structures share and express. In the same way we can come to appreciate the common spiritual dimensions of each religion's differing metaphysics and theology: While the several traditions give different answers to the question of the meaning *of* life, they provide a multiplicity of guidelines and spiritual disciplines to enable everyone to find meaning *in* life: in this world. By plumbing the spiritual depths of other religious traditions, then, we may come to explore more deeply the spiritual resources of our own, and at the same time diminish the otherness of the other and create a more peaceable and just world in which everyone can find meaning in their all-too-human lives.

ABOUT THIS VOLUME

Against this background we may turn more directly to the present work, the inaugural volume in the series, *Shinto: The Way Home*, by Thomas P. Kasulis. It is a most appropriate first offering. Shinto, arguably the least well known of the Asian religious traditions, is commonly thought of as applicable and important only to the Japanese people. It is indeed a uniquely Japanese expression of spirituality, but Kasulis does a splendid job of making the tradition come alive for everyone. He does this not only on the basis of solidly grounded scholarship—he is a well-known and highly respected author of many works on Japanese philosophy and religion—but also by sharing with his readers his personal efforts to understand and appreciate the Shinto way of looking at, and being in, the world.

By his efforts he opens the door—or, better, bids us pass through the *torii* gate—to enter into the realm of nature as it has been experienced by the Japanese since the earliest days of their history. Central to these experiences is the concept—and felt presence—of *kami*: the "spirits" that invest every tree, rock, flower, mountain, river, and other natural object. The combined scholarly, philosophical, and personal dimensions of Kasulis' narration of Shinto beliefs and practices make it extremely difficult for even the most skeptical of readers to dismiss this spiritual orientation toward nature as simple pantheism. Instead he invites us, too, to experience the *kami*, which we might do by looking closely, in wonder, at the intricacy of the petals of a flower, or contemplating the spreading shadow of a tree, or feeling the awesome majesty of a mountain waterfall. Perhaps we may all, not alone the Japanese, experience nature as *kami*-filled.

In addition to inviting his readers to attend seriously to the unique Shinto expression of Asian spirituality, Kasulis does more. It is fairly well known that in addition to its purely religious dimensions, Shinto was enlisted to serve in support of a nativistic political and military effort to subjugate the peoples of Asia, culminating in the horrors of the Sino-Japanese War and later (after Pearl Harbor) World War II. Although the militarists/nationalists claimed to be liberating other Asian nations from the evils of Western imperialism, the imperialism they put in its place was at least equally, if not more, brutal and oppressive. By clearly distinguishing purely spiritual Shinto from its untoward political employment—existential Shinto and essentialist Shinto in his terms—Kasulis enables his readers to learn from and celebrate the former while warning against the dangers inherent in the latter.

There is much more in this wonderful little book than has been noted here, but perhaps enough has been said to prepare the reader for the spiritual journey to follow. The *torii* beckons.

HENRY ROSEMONT, JR.

Preface

This book originated at a party. During the East-West Philosophers Conference held in Honolulu in January 2000, a small number of us philosophers were gathered in Henry Rosemont's temporary quarters at the East-West Center's Lincoln Hall. Henry is both an old friend and respected colleague, not to mention most gracious host. As the party was winding down and people began to disperse, he asked me to stay for a few minutes to discuss something. As the two of us sat down—Henry with his beer and I with my scotch—he explained that he had just signed a contract with the University of Hawai'i Press to edit a series on "Asian spiritualities." He invited me to contribute a book to the series and, knowing my writings on East Asian Buddhism and Japanese philosophies, suggested several good topics.

At one point, though, I suddenly chimed in with "what about a book on Shinto spirituality?" Henry's eyes sparkled. We spent several minutes discussing the nature of the book and what it might try to accomplish. In the past two decades or so, Western scholars have analyzed Shinto fruitfully in various ways: historically, anthropologically, textually, and ideologically. What if one started instead with a philosophical analysis of Shinto spirituality and from this point of departure then considered everyday practices, historical developments, textual readings, and political ideology? Might we see something new that the other perspectives had overlooked? As I walked down the hall to my room, a mental kaleidoscope configured and reconfigured ideas, images, memories, texts, and observations. When I finally got to bed, I lay there quietly so I could drift off to sleep. The light rain plip-plopped on broad tropical leaves outside my open window and an occasional breath of wind eerily rustled the leaves outside and curtains within. Now and then the moon would peep from behind the clouds to cast a haunting blue-gray sheen on the objects around me. There is a term for such weather in Japan—*ugetsu* (literally "rain and moon")—and it is often used in reference to spooky or ghostly tales.

Then a thought disrupted the dreamy drifting: what had I just done? In my career I have never written extensively about Shinto. I teach about it in my religion courses and address it in my writings, but never as a main focus. I am primarily trained as a scholar of Japanese philosophy and there is simply not that much Shinto philosophy to talk about. Now queasy about what I had just gotten myself into, I tried to fathom why "Shinto spirituality" had spontaneously popped up in my mind as I was talking to Henry earlier that night. Maybe it was the conviviality of the evening: being together with old friends, discussing our work and personal lives. Maybe it was the aroma of the seaweed-wrapped rice crackers at the party, a scent that always whisks me off to Japan. Maybe it was the surroundings of the University of Hawai'i where I had begun my study of Japanese philosophy and culture and had later taught it for five years. Maybe it was just the scotch. The source of the idea still a mystery to me, I let it go and started to drowse again—surrounded by the sound of raindrops and wind, the ghostly shadows of the moon. Somehow I now felt at peace with my not knowing the mysterious origin of my suggested topic. At home with the idea of writing about Shinto spirituality, I slipped unworried into deep slumber.

This narrative of origins befits a discussion of Shinto spirituality. Shinto can be an antidote to an overly robust drive to explain everything and to assume that what cannot be fully explained must be unreal. Suppose someone experiences something weird, mysterious, and powerful, albeit inexplicable. Should that person deny the experience so long as it is not explained? Or simply accept the experience as unexplainable? Shinto spirituality raises such questions.

This book describes some spiritual experiences common in Shinto and traces relations between these experiences and several historical, social, political, intellectual, and cultural aspects of Japan that influenced Shinto's becoming the religion it is today. The analysis, therefore, is twofold: it delves first into the nature of certain human experiences and, second, into the religious significance of germane events in Japanese culture from prehistoric times to the beginning of the twenty-first century. Although the size and purpose of this book necessitate a much abbreviated account of these developments, the bibliography directs readers to important studies in English that can enrich their understanding of many details only introduced here. The point of the present work is not to explain or describe Shinto fully but to give readers a feel for it. Perhaps this is why the idea of a book on Shinto spirituality seemed so important that mysterious night in Hawai'i. Most books on Shinto understandably focus on one aspect of the religion: its festivals and rituals, its relation to modern Japanese politics, its role in intellectual history, its relation to Japanese identity, its institutional structures, and so forth. This book, by contrast, tries to give readers a philosophical orientation that will allow them to see how these aspects of the religion fit together. It is not meant to be conclusive—quite the opposite. Reading this book should help readers begin, not end, their study of Shinto. It is a book that opens into other books.

Acknowledgments

First I wish to thank Henry Rosemont of St. Mary's College and Patricia Crosby of the University of Hawai'i Press for undertaking this new project, a series on Asian spirituality, and for inviting me to participate in it with this volume. Henry's comments on the manuscript's first draft helped shaped the book in profound ways and Pat's constant encouragement kept the project on track. I am also grateful the press arranged for Don Yoder to copyedit the text. This is my third book to benefit from Don's keen eye, attuned ear, and sharp pencil. Second, I want to thank scholars of Japanese religions, both Western and Japanese, for their crucial contributions to this field, especially in the past two or three decades. Many have made efforts to give us a truer picture of this important religion without the ideological biases, both in Japan and the West, developed during the war years. Without their incisive analyses, I doubt I would have found Shinto interesting enough to write about in the way I have. On a few troublesome points, I especially valued the input from Michiko Yusa of Western Washington University, who was kind enough to serve as a reader for the manuscript. Although I have not been able to incorporate all her suggestions successfully, the manuscript was improved significantly by her comments. There may remain errors of which I am not aware and for that, of course, I am solely responsible. Furthermore, in such an introductory book there will always be some generalizations lacking nuance. I have recommended at the end some readings available in English that address particularly well certain details I was obliged to omit. The list is not meant to be comprehensive in any way; it is only a guide to where interested readers might turn next.

Third, I would like to thank the National Endowment for the Humanities for supporting my research in the history of Japanese philosophy with a 2000 Summer Grant for University Professors and a 2001 Research Fellowship for University Professors. A large portion of the historical overview of Shinto in chapters 3, 4, and 5 is an outgrowth of that research. This book is the first direct benefit of that grant and will be followed with a longer, more comprehensive survey of Japanese philosophy in its various forms: Buddhist, Confucian, and modern academic, as well as Shinto. I am also grateful to my home institution, The Ohio State University, for a grant-in-aid that enabled a last-minute research trip to Japan at that crucial point when I was just finishing the manuscript.

Most of all, I wish to thank my wife, Ellen, for her continued loving support. She has always been my personal way home and she is the holographic entry point through which my whole world is reflected. This book is dedicated to her.

Introduction

Shinto is particularly difficult to explain, even for most Japanese. Because its basic values and patterns of behavior have filtered into Japanese culture as part of tradition, most Japanese seldom reflect on Shinto as a "religion" in which they consciously participate. For them, being Shinto is neither a set of beliefs formalized into a creed nor an identifiable act of faith. Its festivals and annual celebrations are things Japanese do because it is traditional, just as some Americans celebrate St. Patrick's Day and Mardi Gras with parades and parties. One does not have to be an Irish Catholic to drink green beer nor practice Lenten abstentions to enjoy Mardi Gras in New Orleans. Analogously, Shinto can be considered merely part of Japanese cultural custom. This is not the whole story, however.

Westerners with some exposure to Shinto know it also as a religious tradition stressing sensitivity to nature, purification, and simplicity. Most foreign tourists to Japan have been impressed with the extraordinary serenity, restrained design, and natural beauty of many Shinto sites. Towering trees, white gravel grounds, carefully pruned shrubs, and beautiful flowers instill peace in many visitors, a peace arising not from an aesthetic flight from the world but from a heightened appreciation and outright enjoyment of it. Boisterous Japanese families with young children and old folks on pilgrimages suggest Shinto not only celebrates life but also brings celebration to life. I have heard many foreigners say they felt oddly at home in such environs. Some who have lived in Japan for some time have gone so far as to say that on many occasions they have "felt Shinto" themselves.

Most people are aware of another dimension of Shinto as well: the Shinto of nationalism, imperial reverence, and ethnocentricity. It is the Shinto of kamikaze pilots and militarist fervor, the Shinto of a divine emperor leading a unique global mission for the Japanese nation and its people. It is the Shinto that dominated the international politics of the first half of the twentieth century.

This book investigates how these aspects—the traditional festivals and rites, the celebration of nature and life, the nationalism and militarism—can coexist in the same religion. Is there perhaps something about the paradox in Shinto that can shed light on other religious traditions as well? Or, on the contrary, is the case of Japanese Shinto unique? In exploring such questions we will examine Shinto *spirituality* as both point of departure and ultimate destination. By framing the discussion in this way, we will find subtle links within the development of Shinto that we might otherwise overlook. There are two warnings, however, about the term "spirituality" as employed in this book. First, the term is not being used to emphasize personal over social or institutional religiosity. Second, the term does not necessarily imply something mystical or transcendent. Let us consider each point briefly.

With respect to the first admonition, when some people hear the word "spirituality" rather than "religion" they think of a religious experience that is especially personal, individual, and outside "organized" religious institutions. Yet reflection shows that spirituality is seldom a strictly private affair. Felt as an inner resonance, spirituality is not an external phenomenon we can study simply by looking at it. Its character emerges only through the intimation of those who share their intimate experiences with us. The neophyte internalizes spirituality by doing what others do and talking how they talk. To express one's own spirituality, one must first be impressed by the spirituality of others. Even the Buddhist or Christian hermit, alone in an isolated cave or cell, sits in the lotus position or kneels in prayer. The hermit did not invent these postures but learned them from someone else. Even in solitude, the hermit reflects a communal context. We must not overlook this vital communal dimension in even the most personal expressions of the spiritual.

The other admonition is not to assume that "spirituality" always implies a belief in something transcendent or supernatural. People sometimes think that spirituality is inherently mystical, a withdrawal from everyday affairs. It need not be so. Whereas any religious tradition may include ecstatic departures from the ordinary, religious people frequently find the spiritual in the most quotidian of human experiences. Spirituality can be like our awareness of light: we might experience it as a blinding, all-encompassing flash or as the medium through which we see the configuration and coloration of our ordinary world. It is the difference between a flashbulb going off near our faces in a darkened room and our being engrossed in the luminescent nuances of an Ansel Adams photograph. Both are experiences of light. Indeed the light of the flashbulb and the highlights on the misty peak of El Capitan are in some respects the same thing—light. Yet the different contexts make for a different kind of experience. So, too, for spirituality. It may appear so intensely and abruptly that it obliterates everything else, or it may be reflected off or refracted through the most mundane events. As we will see, Shinto spirituality most often takes the latter form. To limit our sense of spirituality to the mystical would be to miss a major part of what it means to be Shinto.

The path we take in this book winds its way in the following manner. Chapter 1 offers an entrance into the spiritual feelings associated with Shinto. Throughout Japan's history, there has been an orientation in living—a manner of feeling about the world and of feeling one's way through the world—that has deeply affected Japanese culture and resonates profoundly with Shinto spirituality. Much of this is not so distinctively Japanese, however, that people from other cultures and traditions cannot empathize with it. Indeed, like other foreigners who have spent time in Japan, I have at times "felt Shinto." This does not mean I *am* Shinto, but I have felt in Shinto settings certain responses congruent with Japanese accounts of their own experience. Furthermore, I suspect similar events occur in virtually every culture, in situations not necessarily associated with Shinto at all. Drawing from my own experiences of the relevant sort, chapter 1 outlines a generalized account of the kind of sensitivities at the heart of the Shinto worldview. The goal is to encourage readers to look for correlates in their own lives—regardless of whether they have ever been to Japan or visited a Shinto site. This approach will give us a foundation for further insights into Shinto's function within Japan.

Chapter 2 takes us from the special event of consciously entering a Shinto context to the less self-conscious spirituality of the ordinary. The more we investigate everyday life, the more we enter into cultural particularities. Whereas chapter 1 addresses Shinto spirituality as an experience not necessarily limited to Japan, chapter 2 explores certain aspects of Japanese daily life insofar as they reflect this spirituality. Incidentally, being Shinto (unlike just feeling Shinto) is almost exclusively a Japanese phenomenon: very few people outside Japan identify themselves as Shinto. When asked in polls or a census, however, the type of data compiled for encyclopedias and almanacs, almost all Japanese (over 90 percent) identify with Shinto. For many Japanese, "feeling Shinto" and "feeling Japanese" are barely distinguishable.

Spirituality, as noted earlier, commonly has a communal setting to nourish it. Where there is community, there is social organization. And where there is social organization, there are institutions. This is certainly true for Shinto. To understand Shinto spirituality fully, we must investigate its social and political aspects. Furthermore, because Japanese social and political organization has undergone radical changes through the centuries, it is not surprising that Shinto has institutionally changed through time as well. In light of this, some scholars have spoken of Shinto in the plural rather than the singular. Prehistoric animistic/shamanistic Shinto, early imperial Shinto, Buddhist syncretistic Shinto, nativist Shinto, folk Shinto, Sect Shinto, Shrine Shinto, State Shinto—all are scholarly designations appropriate to certain contexts.

To delve deeper into the cultural contexts of the religion and probe into why at times there seem to be multiple kinds of Shinto, we will explore the tradition at various points in Japanese history. Chapters 3, 4, and 5 survey this history, especially in terms of doctrines and institutions. As we will see, Shinto is a religion with roots going back to Japanese prehistoric times. But in another sense, it is also a religious tradition whose "history" really begins sometime around 1801. This somewhat arbitrarily chosen threshold marks the death of Motoori Norinaga, an intellectual who gave Shinto a new footing, a basis that after his death became the foundation for a new (or almost new) kind of Shinto institution.

This is an appropriate point to introduce a distinction that will serve us well in trying to understand the evolution of Shinto. It arises from our concern about what it means to identify oneself as "Shinto." We will distinguish two kinds of spirituality: existential and essentialist. The first proceeds by finding an appropriate label for what a person values, believes, and does. "Because I behave or feel in such-and-such a way, I am Shinto," for example. We can call this an "existential" Shinto spirituality. It is a self-identity that arises from naming a way of living: the patterns of one's existence in the world. The second type of spirituality arises from an intuition about an inner core of one's being —one's essence, soul, or innate character—that defines or drives one's values, beliefs, and actions. "*Because* I am Shinto, I behave or feel in such-and-such a way." We will call this an "essentialist" Shinto spirituality because one's identity as Shinto precedes and determines (rather than merely names) one's patterns of religious behavior.

The difference between an existential and essentialist spirituality is subtle. Indeed, on the surface, a person who identifies with Shinto in one manner may be virtually indistinguishable from one who identifies with it in the other. Yet as will become increasingly clear as the book proceeds, how people identify with a religion can profoundly affect how that religion functions within a society. For an initial glimpse of what is at stake, let us consider the difference between an existential and essentialist form of identity in an example that has nothing to do with religion.

Suppose there are two comments people commonly make about Mary: (1) "Mary tells a lot of jokes" and (2) "Mary is a comedian." What is the connection between the two statements? There are two possibilities. One is that Mary typically jokes about matters and, to classify this pattern of behavior, people call her a "comedian." In this case the word "comedian" *describes how* she frequently acts and speaks. As such, her being a comedian is an existential identity. The other possibility is that Mary is by nature a comedian—and because she is a comedian, she thinks, feels, and acts in certain ways. If this is the situation, then her being a comedian is an essentialist identity: it *explains why* Mary behaves as she does. If she is going to be true to who she really is, she should let her comic nature guide how she acts. A key difference between the two ways of being a comedian hinges on the causal connection between the two statements (1) and (2). If the relation is that (2) is true because of (1), the situation is existential; if (1) is true because of (2), it is essentialist.

In summation: if we know Mary is existentially a comedian, we know something of her style or manner. We know about how she has chosen to interact with others. If we know Mary's being a comedian is essentialist, we know something about her basic nature that causes her to behave in certain ways. Different expectations derive from the two modalities. Suppose Mary tells lots of jokes but is also an accomplished pianist. If her being a comedian is existential, we cannot by knowledge of this fact alone predict how she performs on the piano. She may be desperately serious when she plays the piano but lighthearted at other times. If her identity as a comedian is essentialist, however, we might reasonably expect that her comic side is evident even when she plays the piano. She may even use a piano in her act at a comedy club.

Let us apply this existential/essentialist distinction to Shinto spirituality. When people say they are "Shinto," are they giving a conventional name for how they happen to think, feel, and act? Or are they designating an essential part of themselves that *leads them* to think, feel, and act in certain ways? If the former (the existential identification with Shinto), the connection with the religion is ad hoc and flexible. Their Shinto spiritual identity would then be a conventional name applying to some of their typical ideas, values, and practices. To change such an existential identity would be akin to a change in preference, taste, or habit. If, by contrast, the identification with Shinto spirituality is of the essentialist form, the situation is more prescriptive than descriptive. Insofar as the essentialist identity is based on people's true nature, they *must* (or should) behave in certain specified ways. The essentialist Shinto spirituality determines and prescribes, rather than simply describes, their thoughts, values, and actions.

Shinto's development as an institution through Japanese history is a tension between these two forms of spirituality. This book contends that at different times one or the other kind of spirituality has tended to dominate. In chapter 3's discussion of Shinto's origins, we find the foundation for both. Chapter 4 then shows how in the millennium from the early ninth through early nineteenth centuries, Shinto took the form that favored a more existential mode of spirituality. Chapter 5 explains how and why this tendency shifted to more essentialist modalities of Shinto spirituality from 1801 to 1945. Furthermore, it explains how the tension between the two kinds of Shinto spirituality remains unresolved in Japan even today. In chapter 6, the final chapter, we will consider the options Japan faces for resolving this tension and also explore some general issues about the interface of existential and essentialist spiritualities in other religious traditions as well. This discussion will give us the opportunity to reflect on what our study of Shinto can teach us about spirituality in general.

A few points about stylistic conventions. First, this book uses the modified Hepburn romanization of Japanese. For readers who would like an approximation of how to use this romanization in pronouncing Japanese terms and names, see the appendix. Following common English usage, the following eight Japanese words have been Angli-

The Great Torii *of Yasukuni Shrine*
A schoolgirl walks home silhouetted beneath a torii *of Yasukuni Shrine*
in Tokyo. Such huge torii *frame the main approach to the central*
shrine building.

cized by dropping the long vowel markers: Shintō, shōgun, Tōkyō, Kyōto, sumō, Honshū, Kyūshū, Ōsaka. Second, the Japanese convention for personal names is to give the surname first and then the given name. This book follows that convention. Third, the Japanese given name may be an acquired name (such as an ordination name or pen name) and Japanese often refer to famous people by that name alone. The haiku poet Matsuo Bashō, for example, is usually referred to as "Bashō," not "Matsuo." This convention too will be followed here.

CHAPTER 1

Entering Through the *Torii*

This chapter takes us into an experience at the heart of Shinto spirituality, whether existential or essentialist. As mentioned in the introduction, one does not necessarily have to be Shinto to feel Shinto. In my visits to Japan and to Shinto environs over the decades, I have had experiences I consider spiritual. When discussing them with others—both native Japanese and longtime foreign residents alike—my accounts of these Shinto-inspired events resemble theirs. Therefore, to add detail to the analysis and also to make the experience of "feeling Shinto" seem less exotic to the Western reader, this chapter includes a few personal experiences of my own. The point is not to claim privileged access to any such spiritual events. Quite the contrary, I wish to exemplify that, however special they might feel, such occurrences are commonplace.

When comparing experiences among individuals or across cultures, we can look at either *what* is experienced or *how* it is experienced. Your favorite food may be chocolate, for example, and mine may be popcorn. Certainly no one would claim chocolate is that much like popcorn, but the experiences of "having a favorite food" may still be similar. Despite the disparity in *what* we prefer, *how* we crave and savor our favorite foods may be alike. In short: because I know what it is to have a favorite food, I can in one crucial respect understand your love of chocolate. This observation is helpful in trying to appreciate the spiritual experience of someone from a tradition other than our own. Although two people from different religious traditions may not agree on what is sacred, how they experience the sacred may nevertheless be quite similar.

When analyzing my own episodes of "feeling Shinto," I find that the how of the experiences is not unique to Shinto or even Japan.

Therefore our entry into Shinto spirituality begins, oddly enough, with experiences not directly related to Shinto at all. The goal is to find a common point of departure even for readers who have never visited Japan or a Shinto religious site.

The Experience of Wondrous Mystery

In many religious traditions—and Shinto is no exception—spirituality resonates with the mysterious and wondrous. To appreciate mystery, one must respond both to it and within it. That is: when we spiritually encounter mystery, it is inseparably about something (the inexplicable) and about how we respond to that something (with wonder). As an object, the mysterious may sometimes seem a potency that is always present but often unnoticed or forgotten. It is like the advice to "stop and smell the roses." We know the roses are blooming, but we may be too busy to appreciate their fragrance. If we take the time to stop and smell them, however, we are reminded of what has been there all along. Sometimes the mysterious is like that forgotten presence. At other times, though, the mysterious may be something new that seems to come forward from beyond the horizons of ordinary experience, calling attention to itself. The mysterious can beckon or even demand our attention. In such cases we are *struck* by it. In either form, the mysterious stirs a reaction: an "ah!" This "ah!" is not an "ah ha!" or "Eureka!"—that is, an exclamation of discovering an answer. The "ah!" response to mystery is more a dumbfounded recognition and appreciation of an inexplicable power or presence. The "ah!" venerates something we do not (perhaps cannot) fully understand. Shinto spirituality treasures the mysterious as something awesome.

Like other people, I have felt such awe, mystery, and power in various contexts, not all of them Japanese. I felt it when driving through the Rockies near sunset and, rounding a bend, came unexpectedly upon a stunning mountain valley. It was voiced as a "Wow!" at my first sighting of Niagara Falls. It was expressed in stunned breathlessness when I visited Makapuʻu Point in Hawaiʻi, agape at the blue expanse of sky and surging sea. I have felt it too when witnessing a toddler's or foal's first steps. I cherish such experiences precisely because they take me beyond the bounds of detached observation. I recognize them as special without the need for explanation. Such experiences resonate with what we are calling "feeling Shinto."

Feeling Shinto is not limited to romantic naturalism, though. It includes even encounters with objects of human creation. I experienced something like it in seeing originals of the Magna Carta and Declaration of Independence or when I heard for the first time the "Kyrie" from Berlioz' *Requiem* or Miles Davis' album, *Kind of Blue.* It has been in the spark shooting up my spine when I enter Ohio Stadium filled with a hundred thousand cheering Ohio State football fans and whenever I see Michelangelo's *David.*

The awe in feeling Shinto is not necessarily comfortable. I experienced a creepy sense of awe when visiting a London alley, virtually unchanged in a century, that had been a mutilation setting for Jack the Ripper. It was also in the hairs standing on the back of my neck when I was a kid walking by a desolate cemetery on a foggy, moonlit light, hearing a rustling from the grounds accompanied by an eerie whistling. The awe was mixed with fear when I stood transfixed, watching a finger of black storm on the Oklahoma horizon reaching down toward the ground, and again when I saw the surf from a tropical storm swell and crash across the Hawaiian road on which I was driving. There was an awestruck shudder in my voice the first time I felt the shock of a northern Wisconsin night having a windchill factor of -90°F.

Most people acknowledge having had such powerful encounters in their lives. The experiences intrigue, startle, or frighten. Shinto spirituality is about learning to feel at home with them—feeling we belong with them and them with us—even if we do not fully understand why. Indeed, to go too far in trying to explain them becomes a way of explaining them away, robbing them of their initial power. Shinto has names for such awe-inspiring presences—whether natural or humanly made, whether associated with joy or fear, whether a site, a personage, or an event. Shinto's name for their vital power is typically "*tama*," "*mi*," or "*mono*." The presence itself is "*kami*." The way to and from this awesome mystery is "the *kami* path": the "*kami no michi.*" The written characters are usually pronounced "Shinto." Shinto springs forth from awe. In ancient Greece some twenty-four centuries ago, Aristotle said that philosophy, too, begins in wonder or awe. Yet his reaction differed from Shinto's. Aristotle hoped to use reason to root out the ground of this wonder; for him, philosophy's purpose was to lead us from awe into understanding. For Shinto, though, the point is to accept the awesome as part of the world in which we live. To deny or try to eradicate the wondrous mystery is no less than to run away from home.

In Futami, on the Japanese coast near Ise, two rocks—about twelve and twenty-five feet high—rise sharply out of the sea a short distance from the shore. A huge rope ties the two together in "marriage." A small Shinto gate stands atop the larger rock, and a larger gate stands on the beach framing the two. Along the shore are various images of frogs, an animal sacred to the place. The Japanese word for frog is *"kaeru,"* a homonym for a word meaning "to return home." These

The Wedded Rocks of Futami
The torii *atop the "husband" rock and the* shimenawa *connecting the "husband" and "wife" indicate the* kami *nature of this natural formation.*

married rocks of Futami suggest two issues for our analysis of Shinto. First, Shinto is about connectedness, the intimate kind of relation in which each related item is part of the other. Second, Shinto designates sites of awe-inspiring power by using markers—in the case of Futami, both the sacred gate *(torii)* and a sacred rope *(shimenawa).* Let us consider each point in turn, beginning with the nature of connectedness.

Internal and External Relations

If two things, call them *A* and *B,* are related, there are two common ways of understanding what this relation means. It may mean that two independent items *A* and *B* preexist the relation and are then connected by some third thing, call it *R,* that makes a relation between them. In this case, if the *R* disappears at some future point, *A* goes back to being just *A,* and *B* to being just *B,* each preserving the integrity of its essential individuality. Philosophers call this type of connectedness an "external" relation because the relating exists outside the intrinsic

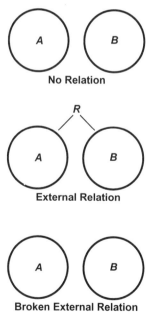

Figure 1. *The Dynamic of External Relation*

character of the two related things. Consider, for example, a foot-bridge connecting two cliffs forming a ravine. If the connecting bridge should ever break, each side would continue to exist independently of the other. The bridge is a relation external to what each cliff is in itself. We can depict such an external relation by Figure 1. If the relation R between the two independent entities disappears, A continues to be A and B continues to be B.

Philosophers call the other kind of connectedness an "internal" (or "inherent") relation. In such a case, the A and B are not independent but interdependent. Item A in its completeness cannot be separated from B in its completeness and vice versa. We can think of an internal relation as two overlapping circles (A and B), and the relation is in their overlap (R). The R is part of A as well as part of B. For this relation to dissolve, therefore, A and B must both become less than what they were before. Consider, for example, a jazz improvisation. Each individual's performance is intimately interlinked with the others' performances. Each musician is affected by and affects every other musician. Figure 2 depicts such an internal interdependence and the result of its disappearance.

The two types of relatedness pertain to the Shinto words for "spiritual power": *tama, mi,* and *mono.* When used in its narrow technical sense, the word *"tama"* refers to a spiritual power infusing a material object while preserving the integrity of both itself and the object. Hence it can sometimes be thought of as resembling the Western ideas of "soul" or "spirit." The relation between *tama* and matter is comparable to the way sand is suspended in the ocean water crashing on the shore. The sand may so thoroughly pervade the waves that we could not get a cupful of that ocean water without its being sandy. Yet the sand does not dissolve into the water. We could take a cup of the water, let the sand settle to the bottom, and count the individual grains. It is a relation in which neither the sand nor the water changes its intrinsic character. Similarly, the presence of *tama* does not change matter, nor does matter change *tama.* Their relation is basically external.

When Shinto discussions focus on spiritual power as internally rather than externally related to materiality, the terms *"mi"* or *"mono"* are often used instead of *"tama."* *Mi* or *mono* do not exist without materiality, nor does materiality exist without them. Neither would be what it is without the other. In this case the relation is not like that between the ocean water and sand but like that between the ocean water and salt. Unlike the sand, the salt surrenders its crystalline structure to dissolve completely into the water. Furthermore, the water in the ocean is everywhere salty. The Shinto terms "*mi*" or "*mono*," when used in distinction from "*tama*," emphasize such an internal relation between spirituality and materiality. They suggest that neither spirit nor matter can exist without interdependence.

Earlier we noted that a wondrous mystery might at times be experienced as something always there but usually unnoticed. *Mi* and *mono* are like that. The material world is at all times in all places spiritual, and the spiritual never exists without the physical. People may become sensitized to this often overlooked dimension of the physical world by engaging in Shinto praxis—that is, its system of interrelated individual practices. We have noted, though, that an awesome mystery may sometimes be something that approaches and calls attention to

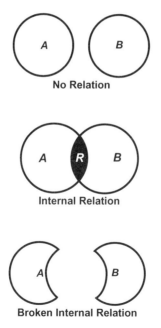

Figure 2. The Dynamic of Internal Relation

itself as well. This is more like *tama,* a spiritual presence with integrity of its own, moving within but not fully disappearing into the physical world. If the integrity of the *tama* is particularized enough, it becomes identifiable as an individuated "soul" or "spirit," *mitama* or *tamashii. Mitama* or *tamashii* can be used to designate something personal such as "my soul" or something collective such as the "soul (or spirit) of the ancient Japanese people"—"*Yamato damashii.*"

To sum up: for Shinto the relation between the spiritual and the material may be external, internal, or both; but the material never exists without *some* relation to the spiritual. Perhaps an electromagnetic analogy will help. Every molecule in a rod of iron contains positive and negative electrical charges. There is no matter without such electrical energy just as there is no matter without *mi*. If this rod of iron is subjected to an appropriate current of electricity coming from outside (like an object being touched by *tama*), the polarities within the molecules go into an alignment such that the whole rod becomes a magnet with its own discernible and discrete magnetic field. The change from unmagnetized to magnetized occurs because of the iron rod's external relation to the electrical current. Internally, however, on its molecular level, the iron rod is always electrically charged. In a sense, the change from unmagnetized to magnetized is not a change in what the rod is, but *how* it is. Analogously, when *tama* "enters" an object, the physical object is not thereby "spiritually energized." Insofar as there is no matter without *mi,* the physical object was already energized. The change related to *tama* lies in *how* the item is spiritually energized.

The term "*mono*" can be used to name yet a third modality. It often refers specifically to a changeling spiritual quality that moves among the forms of ghosts, goblins, animals, and humans. As such it may play a role in spirit possession and be so particularized as to resemble *tama.* Because they differ more in mode than essence, these three Japanese terms—*tama, mi,* and *mono*—tend to blur into each other. For the sake of convenience in this book, we will follow a popular tendency among the Japanese themselves and use the term "*tama*" in its broadest sense to embrace all the various meanings of spiritual power, including "*mi*" or "*mono.*" In those cases where the distinction is crucial, of course, we will be more precise.

Let us return to the two rocks at Futami. Is the relation between the rocks internal or external? At first glance, it might seem the two rocks initially existed independently and then were married by the villagers. In this case the sacred rope would be like a wedding ring signifying the establishment of an external (even contractual) relation between the rocks. On a deeper level, however, the villagers recognized that the connection between the two rocks was *always* there and hence the rope celebrates, rather than makes, the relation. In this understanding, the rope is more like an anniversary ring than a wedding ring. The rope is not a sign that two discrete things have joined in an external relation. Instead it is a sign that the local people recognize the two rocks to have always been married. It is as if the two rocks share a power between them like the shared love of a married couple. Neither rock could be fully what it is without the other. On this deeper level, there are not three items at Futami: a rock, a rope, and another rock. There is just one thing: the *tama* stemming from the overlap of the rocks, the rope, and even the villagers. This brings us to the second point about Futami—the role of *shimenawa* and *torii* as markers.

Shimenawa *and* Torii

In general, Shinto maintains that human beings are internally related to *kami* and without this relation people would not be what they are. The other side is just as important: it is in the inherent nature of *kami* to be interdependent and intimately connected with the world, including human beings. As we will see in chapter 3, according to ancient Shinto myths the world came about as much from the celestial *kami*'s parthenogenesis as by any other means (creation out of a primordial ooze, the progeny from intercourse among the *kami,* and so forth). Thus the world is filled with *kami* and charged with *tama,* but not because the physical world exists in itself and *kami* are somehow connected to it. Nor is it *kami*-filled and charged with power simply because the *kami* created the world. Instead the world is *kami*-filled because the world and *kami* are so interdependent as to be incomplete without one another. Let us apply this belief to the use of the *shimenawa.*

When walking through the forests of Japan or even urban sacred sites, one often comes across a large tree whose trunk is girded with a *shimenawa*. This sacred straw rope demarcates it as *kami*. It is not quite right to think that a *kami* simply inhabits the tree. Such a limited view understands the physical tree to be one thing, the *kami* another, and the latter as somehow residing within the former. Put this way, the relation between tree and *kami* seems only external; one can analyze each separately and then puzzle over how they got related. Extrapolating from our discussion of *tama* and *mi*, however, even when a *kami* is thought to inhabit a tree, it is not that the material tree thereby becomes spiritualized. Because of the omnipresence of *kami*, the tree was always spiritualized. Like every other item in the world, the tree is internally related to *kami*. If there is a distinct *tama* presence, it can inhabit the tree only because the tree is already spiritual as well as material. As important as it is to say there would be no world without *kami*, it is equally important to mention that given the nature of *kami*, the material world *had* to be. The material world consists of bits of *kami*. Matter was not created by an immaterial god. The world as we know it is not separate from the inherent nature of *kami*.

Like the *shimenawa*, the *torii* or Shinto gate is another sacred marker. The *torii* functions as a bookmark for connecting people to awe-inspiring power. It marks where one left off and where one will want to return. It is a tangible gateway to an intimacy with the world, one's people, and oneself. When people get lost in the details of everyday life, when they disconnect from their capacity for awe, they often feel homeless. The *torii* shows the way home. (Recall the frogs of Futami whose name reminds the Japanese of the verb meaning "to return home.") To "get lost" in Japanese is "*michi o machigaeru*," literally, "to mistake one's path." Shinto is the *kami* path and when people deviate too far from it, they lose part of what they are and become lost. Disoriented, they seek a marker to show the way back to the *kami*-filled, *tama*-empowered world. The *torii* serves that purpose. Passing through it, one is on the way to being once again empowered.

Torii and *shimenawa* function in at least two ways. First, they specify a particular place or object as having the concentrated power connecting people with the *kami*-filled world. We have discussed the *shimenawa*'s use to single out a special tree or rock as *kami*, for example. The *torii* most often serve as entrance gates to Shinto shrines, but their use is not limited to this. On a trail up Mount Fuji, for example, as one

A Kami *Tree*
The shimenawa *encircling the trunk and the small wooden sign*
in front of the tree identify it as kami.

nears the top, one may find a simple, weathered *torii* along the route even though no shrine is in sight. Nothing else is around it but the barren pumice gravel below and the empty sky above. This is because Mount Fuji itself is *kami:* the locus of mysterious power and awe. Unlike many holy sites from other religions—Jerusalem, Mecca, or the Buddha's *bodhi* tree, for example—Mount Fuji was not sacralized by a historical event. It is, and always has been, intrinsically awe-inspiring, a site filled with marvelous power. For Shinto, a tree or rock may be *kami* simply by virtue of its age or eerie shape. If people can feel its concentrated material energy, this is enough to associate it with *kami*. This makes it akin to some of the awesome American natural phenomena discussed at the outset of this chapter.

Sometimes the *torii* or *shimenawa* do mark a site having historical significance. A sacred tree, for example, may be *kami* because it was planted by an emperor or empress, who are themselves *kami*. Similarly, a shrine may be dedicated to the *mitama* or spirit of an awe-inspiring, deceased warrior or shogun. Even this person's sword might be *kami*. Such phenomena suggest that something may be *kami* by association. But in understanding this phrase "by association" it is important to think in terms of internal relations. The sword is internally related to the awe-inspiring warrior. It is as much a part of the charismatic warrior as his body. It was not a piece of property over which he held title but a part and extension of who he was. And the power of the sword cannot be separated from the warrior who wielded it. The emperor's tree or the warrior's sword was not endowed with *tama* by someone. Rather, the contact itself made it *tama*. It is analogous to how fresh water becomes salty when it comes into contact with the sea. Once the relation occurs, the fresh and salt water cannot be separated from each other.

The second function of Shinto markers like *torii* and *shimenawa* is their capacity to connect the specific to the holistic. In systems stressing the intimacy of internal over external relations, we sometimes find a phenomenon we might call the "holographic entry point." Systems of external relations tend to emphasize the whole as constituted by the independent parts connected together by external connectors: the whole consists of *A, B, C, D, . . . ,* and the relations—the various *R*s— binding them from outside. To see the whole, one needs to take a vantage point distant from and outside the system. From there the whole appears as a network of parts connected by external relations. See, for example, Figure 3. Systems of internal relations, by contrast, typically think of the whole as intrinsically connected with each part—something more like Figure 4. Yet even this diagram is not adequate since it still suggests the whole consists of its parts but does not show that the whole is *in* every part. In a system of fully realized internal relations, the whole is like an image in a holographic plate where each section of the plate contains the whole image, albeit at a low resolution. Thus we will use the term "holographic entry point" to refer to any phenomenon through which we become aware that the whole is reflected in every part. (See Figure 5.)

For another example of this whole/part relation, think of the relationship between the human body and DNA. Ordinarily a strand of hair is just a part of what a person is. In a forensic investigation, however, this single strand of hair reveals the basic pattern of the whole person's genetic constitution. All of the physical body—not only hair but also eye color, height, body shape, blood type, and even suscepti-

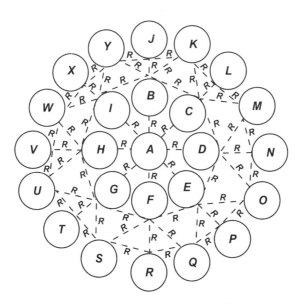

Figure 3. Externally Related Whole

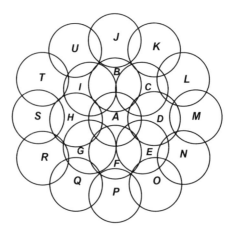

Figure 4. Internally Related Whole

Figure 5. Holographic Whole

bility to certain diseases—is blueprinted in every single cell of the person, including the cells of that strand of hair. The part reflects the whole; the whole is in every part. To see this form of connectedness, the vantage point is not at a distance but through close examination of a single piece of evidence. This bit of evidence functions as a holographic entry point opening to a grasp of the whole.

The *torii* frames such holographic entry points. Insofar as the whole world is *kami*-filled and *tama*-charged, of course, every single thing in our world in some way reflects the wondrously mysterious power of *kami*. Yet Shinto uses markers to designate specific sites where the holographic nature of *kami* is easier to sense. These sites, often set off by *torii* and *shimenawa,* somehow manifest the presence of *kami* more explicitly than do other sites. Thus the significance of Mount Fuji, the married rocks at Futami, even the emperor himself, is not that they are merely isolated sites of *kami*—to the contrary, they are holographic entry points for experiencing *kami* everywhere. By entering the specific, the person's holographic relation to all reality becomes manifest.

As a holographic entry point, the *torii* does not function automatically. It does not demarcate something external into which I can simply tap. To function properly, the mysterious power beyond the *torii* must be in an *internal* relation with the person passing through it. Its power is interdependent with what the person is. If your mind is befuddled and clouded, if your heart is defiled and disingenuous, passage through the gateway will only return you to that. A symbol sacred to Shinto is the mirror. In fact, in many shrines, large and small, major and minor, the altar contains nothing other than a mirror. Along with the sword and comma-shaped jewel, the mirror is part of the official regalia of the emperor as chief priest of the tradition. A mirror's capacity to reflect depends on its cleanliness. Hence Shinto sites usually have a water trough for purification near the entrance. As people enter the heart of the shrine, they are expected to wash their hands and mouth, cleansing themselves of any pollution from physical or verbal misdeeds. Washing away dirt from the journey, they are ready to be at home in the *kami*-filled, *tama*-empowered shrine. Their hearts and minds are pure. Even the *torii* along the path on Mount Fuji serves a similar function. The *torii* reminds pilgrims to cleanse their inner self in preparation for approaching the peak.

Makoto no kokoro

The pure heart and mind we have been discussing is called in Japanese *"makoto no kokoro"* or elided into simply *"magokoro."* *"Makoto"* means "truth," "genuineness," or "sincerity," that is, being as one truly is. Because of my internal relatedness, some of what I am extends beyond the ordinary sense of "me." As a human being in the land of *kami,* one is a portion of the sacred; one is an intrinsic part of the *kami*-filled, *tama*-charged world in such a way that, if the person is pure, he or she mysteriously mirrors that whole. To be genuinely receptive to the presence of *kami* and responsive to it, to make full use of the holographic entry point, people must first be *makoto.* Only then can they recognize how *kami* is part of what they themselves are. They will reflect *kami* and not merely reflect on *kami.* The second part of the term, *"kokoro"*—the "heart and mind" that is to be genuine or true—requires special attention.

As the seat of both feeling and thinking, *"kokoro"* is commonly translated into English as "heart and mind." Understandably scholars often associate the term *"kokoro"* with single words in the Western tradition signifying "heart and mind" such as the ancient Greek *"psyche,"* the Latin *"anima,"* and the German *"Geist."* These Western terms, however, are just approximations, not equivalences, to *"kokoro."* The major qualification is that the Western terms have traditionally been used in contrast to materiality or to the body (the somatic). As seen in its understanding of *kami,* by contrast, Shinto typically considers the material (which includes the somatic) as interdependent with and inseparable from the spiritual (or even psychological). So it is misleading to think of *kokoro* as equivalent to "heart and mind" if this equivalence limits *kokoro* to the psycho-spiritual or to the affective-intellectual, thereby excluding the somatic and physical. To clarify the Japanese concept, let us contrast responsiveness based on *kokoro* with the familiar scientific model of stimulus/response. In the stimulus/response paradigm, "external" things impinge on a person's sense organs to yield physical sensations that, in turn, the mind (brain) processes "internally" as perceptions, relating them to other objects of thought and feeling. Then, goes the model, the process reverses, and through these internal perceptions, thoughts, and feelings the person reacts to the external physical stimulus. Notice the external relations in this model. The world and person exist independently and the stimulus/response mechanism is a twofold pathway connecting two discrete entities.

The traditional understanding of *kokoro,* however, regards it as a resonant responsiveness *within the overlap* between the world and the person. The *kokoro*'s response is an engagement arising from being among things. Whereas it is certainly possible, as the stimulus/response model exemplifies, to distinguish the world and the person as two independent entities, Shinto instead emphasizes the world and the person as interdependent poles within a single field of resonance. Consider how one might respond to an awe-inspiring tree, for example. As we noted earlier in our discussion of the experience of mystery, the awe is not simply in the person or in the tree but in their interaction. The tree must somehow be extraordinary; its *tama* must catch the person's attention (the *shimenawa* helps this happen); but by the same token the person must also be willing to be drawn into this context. If you are lost in thought about something else or are running through the woods to escape a bear, you may not be sensitive to the tree as a holographic entry point. Under the right conditions, though, the *shimenawa* both embraces the tree and ropes the person into an internal relation with it. In short: *kokoro* suggests an affectively charged cognitivity. Thinking and feeling occur together in the person's engagement with the awe-inspiring tree.

Thus *kokoro* is not simply a center of responsiveness within the person. If one has to try to find a single English translation, the "mindful heart" might be a bit closer to the mark—especially if we remember that the mindful heart is not separate from the body. Because the mindful heart is an interdependent complex of responsiveness, *kokoro* can never be just a blind emotion. To the contrary, *kokoro* is cognition with affect, affect with cognition. It is, in this respect, both subjective and objective. To experience the extraordinary, one has to be open to being affectively touched by the phenomenon and its *tama.* Yet one cannot even recognize something as "extra-ordinary" without cognitively comparing it with the "ordinary." Reminiscent of our account of the two rocks at Futami, it is as if *kokoro* is the field between the person and world, those two being distinguishable only as the poles between which the *kokoro* resonates. The awe-inspiring world and awe-inspired self exist only as parts of a single event. To flesh out the idea of *kokoro* still further, let us now consider how one major Shinto philosopher, Motoori Norinaga (1730–1801), explained the role of *kokoro* in creative verbal expression, the point where the poetic and the sacred meet.

First, given the overlap of materiality and spirituality in Shinto, it is not surprising that Norinaga assumed objects, not just persons, have *kokoro*. After all, if physical existence is also spiritual existence, if the world consists of bits of *kami*, there must be the "*kokoro* of things," the "*mono no kokoro*." From an ecological perspective (befitting intimate systems of internal relations), things are interdependent with and responsive to each other. In this interdependence we find their *kokoro*. Second, human beings have *kokoro* as well, but because we have intentionality we can defile its reflective quality. The mirror can be so covered with the dust of everyday worries and problems that it ceases to reflect the *tama*. Norinaga's term for the pure, sincere, mirrorlike human *kokoro* is *makoto no kokoro*: the "true" or "genuine" *kokoro*. Third, along with the *kokoro* of things and of the person, Norinaga drew on classical Japanese poetics to add yet another strand to the *kokoro* nexus: the *kokoro* in words. Norinaga maintained that in ancient Japanese words—that is, the language before Chinese and Korean literary influences—there was not only physical sound but also an accompanying spiritual dimension. That is: "words" *(koto)* have *dama* (variant of *tama*): "*kotodama*." This is the *kokoro* of words, the "*koto no kokoro*."

Applying Norinaga's theory, then, what happens when a poet writes a classical Japanese poem about, say, the mist on the mountains? If the poet's responsiveness is genuine—that is, if there is *makoto no kokoro*—the poet's *kokoro* resonates with the *kokoro* of the actual mountain mist and the *kokoro* of the Japanese words. Through the interpenetration and common responsiveness of these *kokoro*, the poem is produced. From this perspective, the poet alone does not write a poem about the mountain mist. More precisely, the mountain mist, the Japanese words, and the poet write the poem together. In a parallel way, if people go through the *torii* and enter the precinct of the *kami* with a pure, genuine *kokoro,* they enter the holographic entry point reflecting the whole in themselves and thereby reflecting themselves into the whole. They feel connected. They feel at home.

Shinto's Identity as a "Religion"

To see how this analysis might help us interpret Shinto praxis, let us consider an example of probably the most common Shinto activity: paying one's respects at a Shinto shrine. We will begin with a description and then follow a few different lines of analysis:

> Suppose we are sitting on a hill in a Tokyo park, not far from one of the commuter train stations used by literally millions of Japanese every day. We overlook a Shinto shrine located in the middle of the most direct path from one sector of the park to the train station. In the morning rush hour, gray-suited businessmen rush through the park to catch their trains and we observe a curious behavior. Some go many yards out of their way to avoid cutting through the shrine precincts. Others take the shortcut through the grounds, but many of this group slow to a walk as they traverse the graveled area of the shrine. Once they hit the grassy region outside the shrine, they again break into a run. A third group behaves differently yet. They reach the grounds and not only slow down but walk up to the shrine building, stop at the trough to wash their hands and mouth, then go up to the shrine, clap their hands, bow formally with hands held together in prayerlike form, clap again, and then leave the shrine grounds. As soon as they leave the precincts, they again break into a run.

Hoping for further insight into the experience of those who stop at shrines in this way, I have at times asked participants a few questions. Often the discussion has gone something like the following:

> "Why did you stop at the shrine?"
> "I almost always stop on the way to work."
> "Yes, but why? Was it to give thanks, to ask a favor, to repent, to pay homage, to avoid something bad from happening? What was your purpose?"

"I don't really know. It was nothing in particular."

"Well, then, when you stood in front of the shrine with your palms together, what did you say, either aloud or silently to yourself?"

"I didn't say anything."

"Did you call on the name of the *kami* to whom the shrine is dedicated?"

"I'm not really sure which *kami* it is."

Such interviews frustrate the philosopher. It seemed my questions were failing to get at what Shinto is and how it functions spiritually for Japanese. From such responses—or perhaps we should say lack of response—to these questions, many commentators on Japan have surmised there is nothing really religious in Shinto at all. That is: if one cannot explain exactly what something is, then perhaps it does not exist. In academic discussions of Shinto, it is not uncommon to find locutions like "Shinto is not a religion but a cluster of folk beliefs and practices," or "a tradition of ethnic and cultural beliefs," or even "a set of loosely connected superstitions." If the commentators want "objective evidence" to support such assertions, they can dredge up abundant survey data to support their characterization of Shinto as nonreligious, at least in the ordinary sense. Let us consider a bit of such evidence.

As we discover from almanacs and encyclopedias published either in Japan or the West, whenever there is a census or survey asking Japanese to check off a box describing religious affiliation, over 90 percent still select "Shinto." Yet some 70 to 80 percent also check off "Buddhist." So, one might reason, because most Japanese find themselves to be both Buddhist and Shinto, perhaps one or both of the two is not a religion at all, at least in the full sense of the term. When commentators take this interpretation, they usually assume that Buddhism is the religion in the pair. (It is found in various parts of the world; it is always included in textbooks presenting a short list of "world religions"; it has a strong textual and commentarial tradition; it has a founder and a clearly defined history; and, perhaps most important, when its practitioners are interviewed their answers are often less cryptic than those of Shinto practitioners.) This leaves Shinto as the "non-religion" in the pair.

Another possibility, of course, is that the Japanese people themselves are not religious at all. Following this line of interpretation, if Buddhism and Shinto are religions, then Japanese do not practice them "religiously." Again there is statistical evidence supporting such a claim. As long ago as the 1950s, in global surveys such as those sponsored by UNESCO, people of various nations have been asked whether they consider themselves "religious." In these surveys, most Japanese have consistently said no. What better proof that the Japanese are not religious—the Japanese themselves say so! Before accepting the survey information on face value, though, we need to factor in problems concerning the Japanese word for "religion."

The Japanese word for "religion" in such studies is *"shūkyō."* There are two points to note about the term's history and meaning. First, this word for "religion" is not an old one. Whereas the *Oxford English Dictionary* cites usages of the English word going back to the thirteenth and fourteenth centuries, for the most part the Japanese word *"shūkyō"* is a neologism of the late nineteenth century devised specifically to translate the Western concept. This means that until a little over a century ago, it was literally impossible for a Japanese to say she or he was affiliated with a religion. There simply was no established word for expressing or even thinking the notion. This suggests that the context for a Japanese person's statement that she or he is "not religious" is quite different from that of a Westerner who is seemingly making the same statement. Westerners who claim to be "not religious" would likely also imply they are not the way most people have been in the history of their culture. When a Japanese says seemingly the same thing, however, the statement does not necessarily carry the same weight since *"shūkyō"* is a modern, not traditional, Japanese idea.

The second point about *"shūkyō"* is the word's etymology. The nineteenth-century Japanese intellectuals who coined the term must have believed there had been no ordinary word in the Japanese language corresponding to the Western noun "religion." Here we find some cultural dissonance, however. When Westerners came to Japan, whether in the nineteenth century or back in the sixteenth (before being expelled), they thought of Buddhism, Shinto, and even Confucianism as religions in the same category as Christianity (or Judaism or Islam, for that matter). Coming from the opposite direction, though, the Japanese intellectuals obviously did not see the similarity. Why not?

From ancient times, the Japanese (indeed East Asians generally) had not missed the point that many of what we call "religious traditions" in East Asia were alike in some fundamental way. In general, the Japanese grouped together the Asian spiritual traditions by giving them names (usually borrowed from the Chinese) sharing one of two suffixes: "*kyō*" (broadly meaning "teachings") or "*dō*" (broadly meaning "path," "way," or "course"). The convention was to precede this suffix with the name for the spiritual inspiration behind the tradition. Thus "*jukyō*" indicated Confucianism ("Confucian scholar" plus "*kyō*"), "*butsudō*" or (later) "*bukkyō*" indicated Buddhism ("Buddha" plus "*dō*" or "*kyō*"), and "*dōkyō*" indicated Daoism ("*dao*" plus "*kyō*"). The name "Shinto" itself consists of the character for "*kami*" (in such compounds pronounced "*shin*") and *dō* (in this case mutated into "*tō*"). In referring to Christianity today in Japan, the common term is "*kirisutokyō*" ("Christ" plus "*kyō*").

As we see in the two terms for Buddhism ("*butsudō*" and "*bukkyō*"), the suffixes "*dō*" and "*kyō*" may be interchangeable. There is, however, a difference in their etymologies: "*dō*" has the nuance of praxis and "*kyō*" of doctrines. Hence the Japanese arts as well as religions may have the suffix "*dō:*" *budō* ("way of the warrior" or martial arts), *chadō* ("way of tea" or tea ceremony), *shodō* ("way of writing" or calligraphy). In self-consciously creating a word to translate the Western term "religion," this difference in nuance between *kyō* and *dō* is relevant. To use *kyō* in *shūkyō* suggests a Japanese impression that the Western concept of "religion" is more about doctrine or creed than practice.

What about the first part of the word, the "*shū*" of "*shūkyō*"? The term "*shū*" suggests a discrete religious community with common practices and teachings. In fact, the term "*shūkyō*" was not truly a neologism. There was a rather arcane Buddhist use of the term to mean specifically the doctrines of any particular Buddhist sect or school. Given this etymological context, to inquire in Japanese whether someone is "religious" *(shūkyōteki)* may seem a little like asking them if they are "sectarian" or "dogmatic." In choosing such a word to designate "religion," the scholars who created the neologism might have been thinking of the evangelical and exclusivist aspects of the Western religions they had encountered (especially through Christian missionaries). This exclusivity in Japanese Christianity continues today, incidentally: the large majority of the 1 percent of Japanese who designate "Christian" as their religious affiliation do not, unlike many of their Buddhist or Shinto compatriots, also select another tradition.

To sum up, then, once we begin to understand the Japanese word for "religion" used in the census and surveys, some of the paradoxes dissolve. If both Shinto and Buddhism are viewed as spiritual paths, Japanese may be comfortable taking either, depending on their destination at the time. Furthermore, following such paths may have nothing to do with an exclusive system of teachings aligning people with one and only one denomination. Perhaps in saying they are not *shūkyōteki*, many Japanese people on some level may be denying sectarianism, exclusivity, and emphasis on doctrine while still affirming a distinctively traditional Shinto type of spirituality—one that understands religious traditions as overlapping, not discrete. Thus the Japanese respondents to a survey may be saying they are not "religious" in the way Christians (as they perceive them) are "religious." In chapter 5, we will examine as well a historical and political reason contemporary Japanese might identify themselves as Shinto even while insisting they are "not religious."

If we want to gauge Japanese "religiousness" without falling into the terminological quagmire of *"shūkyō,"* how might we pose the question on a survey? When this issue came up in a graduate class almost thirty years ago, our professor playfully offered a Japanese question that, translated literally, means "Have you worshiped a fox in the past twelve months?" He speculated that probably 90 percent of the Japanese would say yes. The professor's off-the-cuff musing is interesting in two ways. First, he pointed to a practice, not a doctrinal belief. Second, the practice is associated more with Shinto than Buddhism. The Inari system of shrines is distributed throughout Japan. (The term "Inari" refers to the harvest *kami* whose special messenger is the fox.) The shrines typically have a sculpture of a fox at the entrance *torii* and many Japanese—in festival, tourist, and pilgrimage contexts—visit the shrines. Many do so, for example, during the time of New Year as a purification rite to start the year with a clean mirror in hopes of an abundant harvest or general prosperity and health. Thus there is an important sense in which Japanese are indeed religious and, at least statistically, most significantly so in the Shinto vein.

In the introduction we distinguished existential from essentialist spirituality. Let us briefly review the distinction before applying it here. An *existential* spiritual identity derives from the attempt to classify or categorize one's values, ideas, or behavior. People of a certain religious tradition tend to act and think in certain ways. When people's attitudes and behavior basically fit that mode (not necessarily perfectly, but in a family resemblance sort of way), they may identify themselves as members of that religion. The *essentialist* spiritual identity, by contrast, arises from an inner sense that one's values, ideas, and behavior manifest a core quality at the heart of one's very being. If one is to be true to oneself, one *must* think and act in various ways. The essentialist spiritual identity, therefore, tends to be more prescriptive than descriptive: one evaluates one's life (and the lives of others in the group as well perhaps) in terms of the standards that one should meet as a member of that religion. Now let us apply this distinction to the businessman we interviewed at the shrine on his way to work.

It is highly likely that if this businessman were filling out a survey about his religious identity, he would check off "Shinto." Why? Because as he thinks about it (which the survey prompts him to do), he realizes that he stops by the shrine almost every day. This in turn reminds him of other Shinto-related events in his life (such as his marriage ceremony's having included the blessings of a Shinto priest). If he happens also to remember his brother's Buddhist funeral last week (Japanese funerals are usually Buddhist) and the family plot in the Buddhist cemetery where his own ashes will someday be placed, our businessman might also check off the "Buddhist" box on his survey. Such reactions would constitute an existential Shinto spirituality. That is: the man would identify himself with "Shinto" because this is the conventional name for some of the things he regularly happens to do.

If the businessman's identity as "Shinto" were essentialist, however, he would be doing what he does *because* he is Shinto. In this case, his stops at the shrine would be something he felt he had to do, at least if he were going to be a sincere Shinto person. When asked his religious identity, there would be no pause in his answer and it would not require reflection. He would take care to perform his Shinto praxis properly, and he would probably have some grasp of the doctrinal analysis of that praxis. He would be concerned if others perceived him as not living his life according to Shinto values. This would amount to his not being "sincere" either to himself or to Shinto. He would probably also be less likely to identify himself as a "Buddhist" as well. Existentially he might occasionally take part in some Buddhist family activity, but essentially he is Shinto.

Let us explore the more likely interpretation—namely, that the businessman's Shinto spirituality is of the existential rather than essentialist sort. If we were expecting him to express an essentialist spirituality in response to our interview questions, we might have left with the impression that his shrine visits are religiously superficial or lacking in spiritual depth. We might have concluded that if he were really Shinto, he would know a lot more about his praxis (such as the name of the *kami* at the shrine) and be able to explain more clearly the rationale behind his behavior. But this attitude tells us more about our expectations than our businessman's spiritual experience. So let us go back to the experiential side of Shinto as we analyzed it earlier in the chapter and try to use it to explain the man's experience at the shrine.

If the shrine is a holographic entry point and the businessman's *kokoro* is pure (symbolized by the washing of mouth and hands), then the visit to this particular shrine opens him to a general connectedness with mystery, power, and awe. In this case, it is not terribly relevant which *kami* is associated with the particular shrine and it is not surprising that he may not even know. The name of the entrance is less important than where it leads: to being in the midst of *tama* and experiencing an energized relation to all things. The man's focus may not have been on the part (this particular shrine and its *kami*), but on the whole it contains.

We also noted that the businessman's behavior is habitual: he said he almost always stops on his way to work. To some people such a routine might suggest the man is "blindly following tradition" rather than being spiritual. Let us not jump to this conclusion, though. In the context of musical performance, the routine of daily practice is usually considered a sign of dedication, not mindless repetition. Similarly, the more often the man feels the spiritual connectedness at the shrine, the more this feeling will carry over into his daily life. The more frequently he reflects the *kami*-filled world, the less likely he will be to ignore it later. Many sensitivities, in fact, deepen with praxis. The more people listen to a kind of music, the more they can appreciate it and the more quickly they can "get into it" when they hear it unexpectedly. The opposite is true as well. Routinization sets the conditions for noticing when things are not as they should be. After years of working with computers, for example, many users, even those not very technically minded, develop a sense for normal computer functioning. When booting up, for instance, they may notice one day that the hard drive sounds "wrong." They may not know if there is a hardware or software malfunction, but they sense a problem. When correctness is internalized, when it becomes part of one's routine, the person is alert to subtle deviations calling for response. In short: recurrent praxis nurtures sensitivity and responsiveness.

Let us now turn to the moment the businessman stood silently in front of the shrine, head slightly bowed, the palms of his hands together in front of his chest. What can we make of his lack of language or conscious thought? If he were really religious, should he not be *praying*? The answer depends, of course, on what exactly one thinks "prayer" means. If prayer means verbalizing one's relation to the sacred or talking to the sacred, then obviously the man is not praying. But if prayer is understood as opening oneself to the sacred or recognizing one's interrelations with the sacred, then the man is indeed praying. Sometimes we think of spiritual quiescence as contemplation or meditation. Maybe the man was contemplating or meditating, rather than praying. Again the issue is what one means by "contemplation" or "meditation." If we think of meditation as meditation *on* something or if we think of contemplation as contemplation *about* something, the case of the businessman does not fit well. Such an understanding of meditation and contemplation assumes an object external to the participant. But as we have seen, in Shinto spirituality the relatedness is often internal, not external. The sacred is approached, not as something out there to be focused upon, but instead as something of which the person is already a part. One might think of contemplation or meditation as not approaching an object but being open or sensitive to what is already present. By this definition, it is fair to say there is something contemplative or meditative in the businessman's activity in front of the shrine. Like the mirror, he is reflecting the spiritual situation but not reflecting *on* it. Hence there is no need for verbalization.

Even if the experience itself is not verbal, it might still seem odd that the businessman found it difficult to characterize it in words even after the fact. If people witness a car accident, they probably do not verbalize the experience at the moment they see it. Yet, certainly, when the police officer later asks them about it, they can "make their statement." That is: they can later express verbally what they originally experienced nonverbally. Nothing could be more common than this. Why, then, is the Shinto man at the shrine so inarticulate about what happened and what he was doing? Perhaps the witnessing of the car accident is not analogous in some important sense. Consider instead a person who has just done something creative. If interviewed after the event, the person's answers might be as cryptic as the Shinto businessman's. Suppose, for instance, we ask poets, musicians, or potters about their inspiration in particular works. We might get an account of the situational trigger ("I was sitting on the beach and . . . ," or "I saw the suffering child on the street and . . . ," or "I was just working the clay and . . . ," or whatever). This describes the context in which the inspiration occurred, but not the inspiration itself. If we pressed for that latter information, we might get a response as vague as "I don't know. The idea just came to me." Inquiring about the exact location on the beach, the medical details of the child's pain, or the chemical composition of the clay would not really deepen our understanding of the creative experience itself. Such questions, like asking the name of the *kami* at the shrine, might convey more contextual information but fail to capture the specialness of the crucial event.

The same analysis applies to the businessman's inability to explain exactly *why* he stopped at the shrine: gratitude, petition, forgiveness, fear of what would happen if he did not, glorification, and so forth. If we go into a church and find a person praying in front of a cross, an altar, or a statue, we would expect the person could tell us in an interview the purpose of the prayer. And, of course, in some cases a person may go to a Shinto shrine with such a specific purpose as well. But this is not the case with the businessman. How are we to understand a practice without a specific agenda? To address this question, we need an analogy different from the Christian praying in a church. Consider this example. Suppose I am out for a summer's evening walk. As I stroll through my neighborhood, I notice the light on in my friend's kitchen and see him sitting alone at the table sipping coffee after dinner and reading the newspaper. He happens to see me through the window and waves hello. I stop to wave back and decide to drop in. He pours me some coffee and we shoot the breeze for a while. Then I get up to continue my walk. As I leave his house, an energetic college student doing a study of neighborhood behavior runs up to me and asks me some questions. Why did I stop at my neighbor's house? Was it to ask for something? Was it to apologize for something? Did I want to thank him for something? Was it to solve some problem between us? Did I think he needed cheering up? None of these characterizations seem to apply. I was in the neighborhood, saw my friend in his house, and just dropped by. I had no particular purpose. I feel good visiting him; I feel at home there, like I belong. I value my relation with my friend and I share time with him.

Applying this thinking to the businessman at the Shinto shrine, we could say he presents a spirituality without an agenda. The way to build an intimate relation is by finding the opportunity to share time together. If parents spend "quality time" with their children, this does not mean that every single activity—playing a game together, taking a trip, having a talk, going to a movie—must have a clearly defined goal. Yet the purpose of all the activities collectively is to nurture the sense of intimate connectedness. If something similar is happening in the case of the man's visit to the shrine, it is no wonder that our interview questions seem strange to him and he cannot readily engage them. Our questions inquire into his spiritual agenda. But in the specifics of the way we put the questions, he has no such clear-cut agenda at all. Such a spirituality without an explicit focus on salvation, forgiveness, enlightenment, liberation, or whatever led an earlier generation of scholars to think of Shinto as "primitive" and "undeveloped," a "tribalism" without doctrine and rationale, a "primal" behavior harking back to the preliterate, prerational consciousness of ancient peoples around the globe. In the final chapter of this book, I will argue that Shinto is not so different from most other religions as it might first appear. Yet because of its particular cultural and historical context, Shinto does foreground an aspect of spirituality often marginalized in other religions and, in particular, by many scholarly approaches to religion. In learning about Shinto, we can also learn *from* it.

With this generalized description of the experiential form of Shinto spirituality, let us now explore some specifics of Shinto spirituality as practiced in everyday life within Japanese culture. What values does it emphasize? When are the Japanese conscious of these values as being explicitly Shinto, and when do they function on a subconscious level? What kinds of ordinary events might make a Japanese feel Shinto? This takes us from the *torii,* a holographic entry point reflecting the whole, down the path to the particularities of Japanese cultural life.

CHAPTER 2

Everyday Connectedness

In the preceding chapter we analyzed Shinto spirituality in its generalized experiential form—thereby establishing a terminology and conceptual framework for the rest of the book. Chapter 1 sometimes used the first person in its phenomenological descriptions for two reasons. The first purpose was to demonstrate there is nothing in the ordinary experience of Shinto spirituality so alien from the experience of most people that they cannot understand it. The type of spirituality discussed in the previous chapter need not be exotic, alien, or simplistic. Second, the first-person anecdotes illustrate how even a non-Japanese might engage the tradition on some level. This point is important because most accounts of Shinto explain it as a *Japanese* religion. Of course, this is true in most respects. Almost all people identifying themselves as Shinto are Japanese; almost all Japanese see themselves as affiliated with it in some way. Shinto was not simply a direct import from the Asian mainland but developed its character within the Japanese cultural and geographical context. In short: as a religion, Shinto is undeniably of and by the Japanese people. Does this mean that the kind of spirituality emphasized in Shinto is for the Japanese people alone? Let us leave this as an open question until we address it again at the end of the book.

Yet the fact that Shinto is practiced as a religion almost exclusively in Japan makes it vital to explore the presence of Shinto in everyday Japanese life. Whatever general spiritual characteristics Shinto might have, we need to understand its particularities as well. Such details take us more deeply into the Japanese culture that has both nurtured, and been nurtured by, Shinto. When considering the function of Shinto spiritual values in the daily lives of the Japanese people, it is helpful to consider two different aspects of ordinary spirituality found in probably every religious tradition as it is commonly lived. The first aspect includes areas of life in which Shinto values resonate invisibly with ways of thinking, speaking, and behaving. For the most part, spirituality in this domain functions as second nature. People are not conscious they are doing anything special. What they think, say, and do is what they have always thought, said, and done. It is the warp and woof by which they weave their daily lives. The second facet of spirituality in daily life, however, is distinguished by an explicit sense of specialness or at least of being self-consciously "traditional"—observing calendrical holidays (such as New Year or various regional festivals), engaging in rituals marking life stages (such as marriage or children's reaching a certain age), or taking journeys to a special place (a famous shrine, for example). This chapter explores both aspects of everyday Shinto spirituality. We begin with the Shinto values that have become second nature to most Japanese.

Rice: A Holographic Entry Point

When Jesus taught his followers to pray, he asked for "our daily bread." Today many people interpret Jesus' use of the word "bread" to mean "food" in general. This reading is probably acceptable, but it drops some of the original cultural context. At the last supper with his disciples, Jesus identified his own body with that bread. Since then Christians have made "breaking bread together" a fundamental ritual of bonding people to God and people to people. For Jesus and the people of his time and culture, bread was the staple of nourishment and the focus of communal eating. On a more mundane level, even today's idioms suggest the fundamental aspect of bread in American culture. "Bread" can be slang for "money" ("Got any bread?"), possibly an extension of the idea of money as "dough." What is basic or fundamental is said to be "bread and butter," and people who pay attention to political pragmatics are said to know "where their bread is buttered." The stomach is referred to as the "breadbasket." Bread is the "staff of life." Yet from the spiritual standpoint, Jesus also reminded people that they "do not live by bread alone." For the Christian, only by being spiritually infused can bread become identified with the "body of Christ," the tissue of Christian life.

Rice has an analogous function throughout Asia, including Japan. An anecdote illustrates the point. While a graduate student at the East-West Center in Honolulu three decades ago, I regularly ate lunch at the center's cafeteria. Every day I would share a meal with fellow students from various parts of Asia and the Pacific as well as the United States. We discussed politics, economics, religion, even dating. The discussions were always remarkably civil, no matter how much we disagreed. Only once did I think fisticuffs might break out. The topic that day? The right way to prepare and eat rice. Somehow the differences in how to cultivate rice (wet or dry rice culture), prepare rice (polish or leave brown), cook rice (boil or stir-fry), and eat rice (with fork, chopsticks, or scooping it up with bread) were paradigmatic to the differences in Asian cultures. The lesson gleaned from that experience: rice may function as a holographic entry into a whole array of Japanese values, especially those linked with Shinto spirituality.

The Japanese may associate tea with Zen Buddhism, but rice is unquestionably the province of Shinto. In a formal ritual, the emperor plants the first rice seedlings of the year; in another, he eats the first grains of the annual harvest. *Sake* (rice wine) barrels stacked on high at Shinto shrines represent (usually symbolically) gifts from donors. At a Shinto altar, rice and *sake* are common offerings to the *kami*. The sacred rope discussed in chapter 1, the *shimenawa*, is typically made from rice straw. Because Shinto and rice enjoy a most intimate ritual connection, it is hardly surprising that as an entry point in Japanese culture, rice carries with it values commonly associated with Shinto as well. So let us examine more closely rice's role in ordinary Japanese life.

A frequent Japanese word for "meal" is *gohan*, that is, "cooked rice." Rice, not bread, can be called the staff of life in Japan. Besides its granular state, it is also pounded into flour so it appears in the form of crackers, noodles, and a gooey dessert or snack called *mochi*. Rice served as the unit of taxation and fiscal exchange for much of Japanese history. For most Japanese, rice has a deep ethnic significance—so much so that the state heavily subsidizes rice farming. Japan might import soybeans, for example, another staple of the Japanese diet. But there would be something amiss, apparently, if Japan could not locally sustain its consumption of rice. Therefore, as passengers zoom along the bullet-train railways linking one Japanese megalopolis to the next, they pass one small valley after another, each populated with hamlets nestled among a sea of rice paddies. Without subsidies and high tariffs on rice imports, such small communities could never survive in today's Japanese economy. Wet rice culture is an inseparable part of much of the Japanese landscape, and for many natives Japan would not be Japan without it.

The Japanese polish their rice to the white luster of a cultured pearl. When preparing it, the cook carefully preserves some of the granules' glutinous coating so the boiled product will be sticky. No individual grain is left unconnected to at least one other grain and, by transitive relation, to all the other grains. At a traditional meal, such rice is usually served in its own bowl of muted elegance or simplicity, unadulterated by contact with other foods. Even when rice is mixed with other foods, it often maintains its character by being the layer underneath the other food. We find this in the various *donburi* (rice bowl) dishes as well as in *nigiri*-style sushi. When rice is stir-fried together with vegetables or meats, the result is generally considered an assimilated form of "Chinese," rather than "traditionally Japanese," cooking. Japanese often eat their rice with disposable (which is to say, virgin) wooden chopsticks. The pair of sticks typically comes stuck together, but the diner (no one else) breaks them apart as if making the utensil out of two twigs from a tree. The most common style of disposable chopstick is rather short and leaves the points square rather than rounded (as is more typical of the Chinese style). The Japanese version is not only more rustic but also more practical for picking up a small or slippery item of food.

The appropriate accompaniment for the traditional meal is *sake*, which is to say, rice wine. Most often served heated to a little above body temperature, its warm flow down the gullet gives the drinker a head start on the "feeling good" function of the alcohol. It is said that the warmth is the most efficient temperature for getting the alcohol into the bloodstream as quickly possible. Unlike Chinese cuisine, the main courses of most traditional Japanese meals are served in individual portions, not family style. The large rice bowl and *sake* pitchers, however, are often left on the table and individual portions distributed as needed. That is: the most communal part of the meal centers on rice and rice products.

If the meal is eaten in a traditional Japanese room, moreover, the diners sit on a tatami-covered floor. Between the outer layers of woven reeds, the filling for the tatami mats is typically composed of straw left over from the harvested rice plants. For the sake of cleanliness, people remove their shoes before stepping on it and the tatami itself lends a subtle scent of rusticity to the room. If the room is in a traditional restaurant, the menu's specials of the day would probably be written in a fine calligraphic hand on a piece of rice paper. Because chopsticks sticking upright in a bowl of rice is an offering to the dead, one takes care not to place them so at the dinner table. It would suggest someone at the table is dead or about to die. In Japanese gangster films, the act can be equivalent to Al Capone's looking someone in the eye and saying "I'm talking to a dead man"—not the best tone for a quiet meal among friends.

The romantic poet William Blake claimed to see a world in a grain of sand. Given its holographic function in Japan, a grain of rice might show us at least something of the world of Shinto. Our description has opened us to an array of Shinto themes: naturalness, simplicity, purity and taboo, purification, separateness and communal solidarity, and intoxication. Let us now explore this cluster of traditionally Japanese Shinto values in more detail by considering them in succession.

NATURALNESS

Naturalness is a prominent theme in almost every serious discussion of Shinto—and rightly so. Many traditional *torii* and shrines of Shinto are made of unpainted wood. (Some were originally painted, but after the paint wore off, someone decided they looked better that way.) The groundcover, if there is any at all, is usually just white gravel, although as a concession to the stability of the visitors' ankles, there may be a paved walkway running through it. There are few adornments in most Shinto sites (although there are many important exceptions—the extravagant Tōshōgu shrine that the Tokugawa shoguns built in Nikkō to honor themselves is probably the most extreme counterexample).

In general, "naturalness" has two senses for the Japanese: either a close connection between humans and nature or the cultivated ability to *make* things natural. The first sense is fairly obvious and follows from the idea that *kami* are an intimate, inseparable part of the natural world. As discussed in the previous chapter, natural objects and events often inspire awe. Certain natural objects may be designated holographic entry points of concentrated *tama*, but for Shinto, in the final analysis, they only help us realize that *all* nature is *kami*. The second meaning of naturalness, however, might surprise some Western readers who think of human artifice as by definition not natural. Yet if we join Shinto in considering human beings as part of nature instead of separate from it, even human inventiveness can be natural—at least if performed with the genuine mindful heart.

Consider, for example, the tatami floor in our description of the traditional Japanese meal. Obviously, tatami is not natural in that it is not found in nature; a dirt floor or even a floor covered with loose straw would be more natural in this sense. Human beings have to manufacture tatami. But the goal is to bring the natural smell, sight, and feel of the straw into the home. The layering of the tatami with its woven, reeded cover makes the straw durable and able to be cleaned in a way loose straw cannot. Yet much of the sensory experience of straw remains. The disposable wooden chopsticks display such naturalness, too. Like many *torii*, they are left unadorned and unfinished. The *snap!* in breaking apart the chopsticks accentuates the point. Though manufactured with machinery, the chopsticks await the personal touch before they are allowed to contact the food.

The rice in the traditional Japanese meal described here was unadorned, too, without any added flavoring. There is a story of two chefs, one Chinese and one Japanese, who were boasting of their respective skills. The Chinese chef was trumpeting his talent for making sauces, using spices, and controlling texture, so that he could make chicken taste like duck. The Japanese retorted he could make a carrot taste more like a carrot than any other carrot anyone has ever eaten. The Japanese chef exemplifies the virtue of "making something natural." That is: the value in this sort of naturalness is not leaving things untouched but working to bring out something of their natural state. Leaving the *torii* and shrine unpainted makes visible the grain of the wood—the natural life patterns of the original tree. To show the naturalness in a manufactured object highlights the shared *kokoro* of nature and humanity.

SIMPLICITY

Simplicity as a primary value follows from Shinto's emphasis on naturalness. Shinto priests and women attendants dress in white with little of the adornment common among the garb of Buddhist clergy. Furthermore, the shrines themselves generally lack the elaborate artistic expressions (paintings, sculptures, statues, gold-leaf furnishings) decorating Buddhist temples. Some Shinto shrines display on the altar no artifact at all, not even a mirror. Indeed, in many Shinto shrines the visitor does not enter the main building itself but stands instead at a gate in the open air in front of it. Furthermore, this outdoor area typically lacks the gardens commonly seen on Buddhist grounds. The natural surroundings of the shrine may be groomed, but the landscaping usually does not have the planned design associated with "Japanese gardens."

In describing rice as part of everyday Japanese life, most of what is "natural" is also simple: the unspiced rice, the unadorned chopsticks, the simple bowls. The best way to make something natural is to keep it simple. The idea is that the natural expresses itself through the simplicity of materials and artist. If simplicity is valued, the natural will be able to express itself most directly through the hands of the cook, the potter, or the chopstick maker. Only the person's *makoto no kokoro* can open itself so egolessly as to create together with nature. The plain clay may speak for itself, but its voice is so soft that the potter of the mindful heart amplifies it so we all can hear it.

Many commentators associate the Japanese emphasis on naturalness and simplicity with Zen Buddhism rather than Shinto. In such books as *Zen and Japanese Culture*, D. T. Suzuki popularized this view in Japan as well as in the West. Suzuki was correct to point out that many arts associated with Japan have a close connection with Zen Buddhism, especially through the tea ceremony and all its accoutrements including ikebana, calligraphy, poetry, gardens, and pottery. Suzuki accurately portrayed Zen's historical significance in the development and institutionalization of these arts. At times, though, he seemed to imply more—namely, that Zen Buddhism *introduced* the aesthetic of simplicity and naturalness to Japan. This claim, if he indeed meant to make it, is wrong.

Simplicity and naturalness were part of Japanese culture and represented in Shinto practices centuries before Zen's emergence in the thirteenth century. The kind of grand simplicity found in many Shinto shrines such as that of the sun *kami* at Ise is an obvious example. Zen prospered through its connection with the Japanese arts, not so much because it was introducing something totally new to the culture, but because it resonated with something old. The so-called Zen simplicity in many drinking bowls used in the tea ceremony, for example, can also be seen as far back as some of the unglazed pottery of the Yayoi period, a millennium before Japanese Zen developed and tea plants were cultivated in Japan.

Small Outbuilding at Ise Shrine
This structure for preserving important properties of the shrine
exemplifies well the Shinto values of simplicity and rusticity.

One can argue, therefore, that the Zen aesthetic was similarly a return to a simplicity predating the Heian court's aesthetic of elegance. This aesthetic of courtly elegance predominated among the aristocrats of the Heian period (794–1185) and reflected the high arts from China, including those from esoteric Buddhism, rather than Shinto. The power of the nobles had waned, however, by the time Zen blossomed in Japan. Zen melded with the Kamakura period's (1185–1333) tendency to go back to the ideals of a simpler, less refined, sometimes even rustic, lifestyle. This aesthetic fit the military mentality of the new political leaders, many of whom had come from the outlands distant from the cultural capital of Kyoto. By this process, Zen values and practices became the center of aesthetic development in the thirteenth through sixteenth centuries.

We can use the example of *nō* drama to illustrate an aesthetic relation between Zen and Shinto. *Nō* (often spelled "Noh") is a traditional Japanese dramatic form known for its wooden masks, solemn chanting, precisely choreographed slow movements, bare stage design, and plotlines of the ghostly or heroic. Such innovators as Zeami (1363–1443) formalized and institutionalized *nō* in the fourteenth and fifteenth centuries, elevating it from folk art to the most rarefied aesthetic heights. In training his actors, Zeami drew extensively from Zen Buddhist principles of discipline and spiritual progress. In so doing, he wove together a distinctive theory of both performance and audience appreciation. Thus it is appropriate to emphasize *nō*'s connections with Zen Buddhism.

Yet we should not overlook *nō*'s relation to Shinto as well. First, the storylines often deal with *kami*, with the transformation between animal spirits and humans, and with the interaction between ghosts and events in this world. These themes antedate not only the introduction of Zen Buddhism into Japan but probably even the formal introduction of any other form of Buddhism as well. *Nō* plotlines often present us with a *kami*-filled, *tama*-empowered world. Certainly many *nō* plays integrate into their storylines Buddhist themes and values as well, but in so doing they reflect the Buddhist-Shinto syncretism so prevalent in the medieval period (see chapter 4). The storylines are not the only obvious connection between *nō* and Shinto, however. For a Japanese audience, the *nō* performance resonates with ritual forms as much Shinto as Buddhist. The *nō* stage has a main section resembling a Shinto shrine, and many outdoor *nō* stages are found in Shinto compounds. The stage, even when indoors, is separated by a small dry moat filled with gravel, much like the gravel in a Shinto precinct. Some movements in *nō* trace back to sacred dance forms, many with ancient Shinto connections. The *nō* music too is historically associated with these ancient Japanese ritualistic dances. The music has unmistakable resemblances, for example, to the ancient court music one still hears in Shinto festivities such as the parade for the Gion festival in Kyoto every summer. For such reasons *nō*—one of the most refined of the Japanese arts—is frequently resonant with Shinto as well as Zen associations in the experience of its Japanese audience.

In summation: it is true that many of Japan's most famous arts flourished because of Zen Buddhism. It is also true that the development of these arts was closely linked to the ideals of Zen training and spiritual cultivation. It is not true, however, that Zen introduced a totally new aesthetic sensitivity for simplicity and naturalness. For the latter, enduring Shinto values have played a crucial role in establishing a cultural basis for the later acceptance of Zen Buddhist ideals.

PURITY AND TABOO

Purity and taboo were two other elements highlighted in our analysis of rice. Purity is a value that obviously complements both naturalness and simplicity. We found purity emphasized in the whiteness of the rice, the use of virgin chopsticks, the rice's not being intermixed with other foods, and the removal of shoes before stepping on the tatami floor. As for taboo behavior, we discussed in the family dinner scene the prohibition against sticking chopsticks upright in a bowl of rice. Forbidden behavior brings about impurity, pollution, or defilement *(tsumi)*. *Tsumi* (or the more ritualistic term, *kegare*) denotes something offensive to be cleansed. If one acts the wrong way in relation to *kami*, the point of connection and overlap between the sacred and the human is itself defiled.

The Western idea of sin generally involves intent; sin usually cannot be accidental. The Shinto idea of defilement, by contrast, is more akin to what we find in taboo cultures—that is, the contact itself is the polluting factor regardless of whether the person knew about the offense or undertook the action voluntarily. In chapter 1 we used the analogy of salt in seawater to exemplify an internal relation. We also noted that if the seawater comes into contact with fresh water, the saltiness diffuses through both. As the positive *tama* of the emperor may diffuse through a tree he planted, so too can something negative pollute a pure mindful heart just by contact. In the symbolic language introduced in the previous chapter, we could say the mirrorlike mindful heart is soiled (perhaps through no fault of its own) and cannot reflect the *kami*-filled world. Things will not go right from this point forward—the only solution is a purification ritual to eradicate the pollution or defilement. Before turning to the purification rituals themselves, though, let us consider in more detail what constitutes defilement. Here we will find further resemblances between the Shinto treatment of defilement and the behavior associated with taboo-based religions.

One of the main Shinto taboos is contact with the dead. In Japan before the eighth century, it was common to build a new palace upon the death of the emperor or empress. The death of the former sovereign was considered so polluting that the successor would want to have a fresh start. Blood, probably as the carrier of life, is a defiling substance when it leaves the body via wounds, disease, or even menstruation. Violating such a taboo calls for purification. In premodern Japan, for example, menstruating women were not to enter shrine precincts and there were purification rituals for women to perform after their monthly cycles. Such rituals are rarely performed today (other than by women having a role in presiding over shrine rituals), but the taboo technically remains. Indeed Shinto tradition dictated that when a newborn was introduced to the *kami* at a shrine, the mother, having been recently defiled by the effluence of her blood in the childbirth, could not attend. The exclusion of the mother at this ritual is no longer the norm—but more by people's ignoring the prohibition than by any official rethinking of the Shinto position.

In summation: if death and menstruation are examples of defilement, or *tsumi*, we can see how wrong is the common translation of "*tsumi*" as "sin," "crime," or even "offense." Death and menstruation are not intentional acts; indeed they are not even avoidable. There is no judgment that *tsumi* suggests moral wrongdoing and, consequently, no issue of forgiveness involved in eradicating it. With its emphasis on purity, Shinto's concern for *tsumi* is mainly an issue of spiritual cleanliness—of cleaning the dust off the mirror of *kokoro*.

The death and the blood taboos also suggest how strongly Shinto is focused on life and its processes. There is a saying that Japanese are born Shinto and die Buddhist. We will explore the Buddhism-Shinto relation more fully in later chapters, but the point here is that Shinto is strongly associated with life: fertility, physical health, creation, and abundance. Therefore its taboos are often associated with its opposite—death. *Tama*, as the life-defining energy, leaves the body at death and the effluence of blood may be associated with this. In fact, the connection between death and blood is so strong that most Japanese films still portray the moment of a person's demise with a trickle of blood escaping the mouth, regardless of the actual cause of death. Blood leaving the body indicates the exit of life-energy.

While discussing the affirmation of life, it is worth noting in passing another common term sometimes occurring in Shinto contexts: "*ki*" (vital force). This term has a long history in China (where it is pronounced "*qi*"), and certainly much of the Japanese notion can be traced there. The meaning of *qi* in China and *ki* in Japan is so extraordinarily complex that we can barely touch the surface of that topic here. In general, we can say *ki* is both spiritual and physical. It is both a force in nature and a life-giving power within humans. It is a matter-energy that is associated in various ways with both breath (or air) and electricity, having applications in both Chinese medicine and physical sciences. The goal in practices related to *ki* is first to recognize its presence, both within and outside oneself, and then to work with it. (The notion of the "Force" in the *Star Wars* films is said to be based on the idea of *ki*.)

Our interest here is that the notion of *ki* sometimes appears in Shinto discourse, especially in the modern period. When it does, it is associated with life and health, both physical and spiritual. In this respect it seems to blur into the traditional Shinto idea of *tama*. Some Shinto-related "new religions" that arose in the nineteenth and twentieth centuries explicitly include the notion of *ki* in their teachings and practices. The term also pervades the discourse of the Japanese martial arts. In fact Ueshiba Morihei (1883–1969), founder of the distinctively Japanese martial art of *aikidō* (the way of mutual harmonization with *ki*) was a member of one of those new religions called Ōmoto-kyō. He explained the origin of his technique as being communicated to him by a *kami*. The training he developed for his students includes Shinto-related chanting and purification rituals.

Finally, given our discussion of rice, it is noteworthy that the Sino-Japanese character used to write "*ki*" has a connection with the character used for "rice." Specifically, the single character for *ki* is composed by combining the character for "vapor" with the character for "rice." (Not all philologists are happy with this common folk etymology, but there is no denying that when anyone looks at the character this is what one sees in its construction.) Thus, on the graphic level at least, *ki* is associated with the steam rising from boiling rice. Anyone who has boiled Japanese rice knows that the released steam is not only water vapor. When it dries, it leaves a sticky residue—evidence that the vapor had been almost invisibly permeated with rice gluten. Pursuing this metaphorical line of thought, *ki* is the invisible nourishing life-force permeating the air and charging it with power. Given their common connections to a universal spiritual/material force, it is easy to imagine how the traditional idea of *tama* and the imported idea of *ki* could become linked.

PURIFICATION

The appropriate response to pollution is purification. Shinto purification rituals commonly involve water, salt, or fire. Of these three, water is the most widely used. In Japan, fresh water comes either directly from the heavens or from mountain streams winding their way down to villages below. Since both the heavens and the mountains are common sites of *kami*, the association between *kami* and water is understandable. In chapter 1's analysis of a typical shrine visit, we mentioned the water troughs used by visitors to purify themselves before approaching the front of the shrine. One of the most dynamic practices of water purification, however, takes place in the ritual called "*misogi*." While walking mountain paths, one may sometimes happen upon a secluded waterfall and witness the ritual. Although it has levels of complexity and variation, the basics of *misogi* are simple. Usually dressed entirely in white, the participant enters a mountain pool at the

Shrine Water Trough
The ladles are lined up ready to be used for washing mouths and hands
of shrine visitors.

base of a small sacred waterfall. With the water pounding down on his or her head, the devotee stands beneath the waterfall and chants a formulaic incantation. Through the *tama* of the sacred water and the *kotodama* (the *tama* of words) in the chant, the person's impurities are washed away.

As we will see in chapter 4, the coalition with Buddhism was important to Shinto's development and it is easy to find practices blurring the distinction between the two. A good example related to purification by water is found at the Temple of Pure Water (Kiyomizu-dera) in eastern Kyoto. This Buddhist temple is probably best known to tourists for its stunning perch on the hillside of Higashiyama. With its main hall standing on colossal wooden stilts to support it on the sharp incline, the temple enjoys a marvelous view of the city below. As the name suggests, however, the site was originally chosen in ancient times for its small waterfall shooting out of a rocky cliff. Today visitors rinse out their mouths with its water or drink it as a purifying act. As was the case with many ancient Buddhist temples, Kiyomizu-dera was built on a site already full of *kami* and energized with *tama*. The Shinto and Buddhist elements are now so interlaced in their internal relations that they are virtually inseparable.

The use of water as a purifying agent is visible, too, in many everyday Japanese practices. A wet cloth is given to diners and travelers to clean their face and hands—a tradition so civilized that it has become a standard practice on many airlines around the world. Shopkeepers typically use a hose or buckets of water to rinse off the sidewalks in front of their establishments at the start of the business day. The traditional Japanese bath has its own rituals of cleansing and purifying. Although neighborhood public baths are rapidly disappearing in favor of baths built into personal homes, some of the traditional protocol is still followed within the household. The order of bathers, for example, may reflect the hierarchy in family relations starting with the head of the household. When entering, each bather first showers off all dirt with soap and water and then, once clean, steps into the hot bathwater to soak. This procedure suggests that the purpose of the bath might be something more than just getting clean. Since the water is often so hot that any movement will sting, the bather sits in the water motionless, relaxing all muscular tension before retiring for the night. The same hot bathwater remains clear for the next person so that family members, one by one, share the same purifying warmth. The experience brings a calm feeling of interconnectedness with the surroundings of home, family, bath, and bed.

At first glance, some of this water-related behavior may seem no more than simple attention to sanitation. Certainly airline passengers using the wet cloths distributed before meals do not think of themselves as doing something Shinto. It is, after all, good hygiene to wash one's hands before eating. Yet the Japanese practices long antedate any knowledge of modern sanitation. Visitors to Japan from China seventeen centuries ago and from Europe five centuries ago commented on the Japanese people's distinctive love of bathing. In Japan bathing is not just to cleanse, but also to purify. Of course, most Japanese do not give such behavior much thought. The Shinto values behind the behavior have become so ingrained that people do not usually reflect on them.

Although water is probably the most common purifying agent in Shinto rituals, salt or fire is also used. Salt is white and associated with the sea and with life. It repels demonic or defiling presences. In the Japanese sport of sumo, for example, the wrestlers use salt in this way. As they approach the ring, they throw handfuls of salt in the air to purify the area of the contest. The Shinto resonances in the ritualistic setting of this sport are unmistakable. In choosing their professional names, the wrestlers usually include references to natural objects such as mountains or trees. The ring itself is marked off by a *shimenawa* shaped into a circle—designating the area as sacred space. The match determines who stays within and who is pushed out of this circle. The sacred nature of the contested space is heightened by the presence of a Shinto shrine roof suspended above the ring. The referee waves a fan to ward off disruptive spirits and signal the stages of the bout. In receiving the winner's prize, wrestlers make a waving gesture resembling that used in Shinto ritual to ward off evils from the four directions. However subliminal some of the symbols may be, the entire event is resplendent with Shinto imagery.

Sometimes fire, too, may be used to purify. Some Shinto festivals feature participants running through the forest carrying fiery torches. Fires of purification in formal Shinto ritual must be ignited from a spark created by rubbing together sticks of sacred wood or by striking a flint. (No matches or cigarette lighters allowed.) The sacred shrine at Ise follows the ancient tradition of using a wooden mortar and pestle. The ignition techniques obviously draw on the idea that the purifying power behind the fire—in this case the spark—is being released from nature rather than created. The fire, therefore, burns off impurities and returns the person to the primordial spark of spirituality always present in nature.

There is one further way of achieving purification—namely, by starting afresh. The disposable chopstick is suggestive of this strategy. When a fork is dropped on the floor, people will get another one that has been cleaned or will rewash the old one. When the disposable chopstick is dropped, by contrast, the person gets a new pair. In Shinto freshness can mean renewal. The chief shrine of imperial Japan is that of the sun *kami* at Ise. To maintain its purity, the old shrine building is dismantled every twenty years and a fresh one erected. This practice is reminiscent of how in ancient Japan, before the eighth century, a new palace was built for each new emperor or empress. In both cases purity is assured through newness.

SEPARATENESS AND COMMUNAL SOLIDARITY

Separateness and communal solidarity, although seemingly opposed, actually work together. The holographic paradigm of the whole-in-every-part makes this possible. In our description of the traditional Japanese meal, each person was served with his or her own portion—rather than with common dishes shared family style as would be expected in a Chinese meal, for example. The chopsticks were to be split apart only by the person using them. Yet the entire setting was in another respect strongly communal—as exemplified by the rice and *sake* being served from a common bowl or pitcher. The Japanese meal is not a group of solitary people who congregate for a collective meal. Unlike the Western notion of society as a contractual connection established among individuals, in Japan people find their solidarity by recognizing the internal relations binding them with others. For Japanese, in being individual one is intrinsically communal: the whole is in every part. This idea is difficult for many Americans and Western Europeans to appreciate, so let us explore it a bit further. A fruitful way to understand this dynamic, especially if we are to apply it to Shinto, is to consider the Japanese interplay between regionality and nationality.

Much is made of the idea that the Japanese are homogeneous or at least see themselves that way. This is only partially true. The Japanese are intensely regional as well. Part of the reason is topographical. Imagine taking a bullet train from Tokyo to Kyoto. Outside the train window, the volcanic genesis of the Japanese archipelago is obvious. A geologically young landmass, Japan is a string of volcanic mountain peaks rising from the ocean floor. Because of its youth, Japan's landscape has not been thoroughly eroded and the mountains drop down rather precipitously into the sea in the vestige of ancient fingerlike lava flows. Most Japanese live in the small plains and valleys between these flows. This pattern is visible as our train passes a succession of window scenery alternating between dark mountainous terrain and bright pockets of towns, cities, and rice-paddied hamlets. If the train were slower and we were observant biologists, we could see that from one valley to the next there is often some variation in vegetation. Each valley is a little biosystem of its own. This is because Japan is generally laid out on a southwest-northeast axis while the major weather patterns are on the perpendicular northwest-southeast axis. (The direction along the axis varies with the season.) Hence the weather fronts hit the coasts and are directed differently into the various spaces between the old lava flows, creating subtle differences in temperature and moisture. Because of these hilly and mountainous fingers, until the development of modern transport systems it was difficult to travel from valley to valley by land. Regional differences in foods, modes of cooking, types of handicraft, and linguistic dialects developed. Regional difference is critical to *sake,* too. There are literally thousands of brands of *sake.* In effect, except for a few national brands, *sake* is a microbrewery phenomenon with the water and fermenting process varying from one region to the next.

Even today the Japanese celebrate their regional differences with television segments on the daily early morning news and talk shows. Each day takes the viewer to a different locale where the commentators report on the local foods, handicrafts, customs, and tourist sites. Department stores and large supermarkets often showcase the goods from a different district of Japan each week. Even the bullet-train staff may sell varying foodstuffs in the aisles as the train travels through the different regions. In short: regional differences are part of Japan's homogeneity. In being regional, the person is sharing in being Japanese. Since the particular reflects the whole holographically, by being regional one simultaneously celebrates the communal whole of Japan. Shinto celebrates this sense of regionality. Most shrines are local or regional, rather than national, in character. The shrines celebrate the *kami* of a particular place or region, yet in so doing they open people to *kami* everywhere. By the special function of the holographic, the more deeply one enters the particular, the more inclusive the connectedness. Therefore one may feel most connected to all other Japanese even when—maybe *especially* when—participating in the most local of Shinto events.

INTOXICATION

Intoxication, the final rice-related theme, arises from our repeated references to *sake* in this chapter. *Sake* plays an important role in Japanese ritual: small bowls are offered to the dead or to the *kami;* a new barrel of *sake* is ceremoniously opened to celebrate the beginning of a new business or political enterprise; and *sake* plays a central role in certain purification rituals. The ancient myths and numerous folktales inform us that the *kami* deities are fond of *sake* and love parties. We have already mentioned that the prominent stacks of *sake* barrels at Shinto shrines symbolize the donations of patrons. In most examples of this kind, one must add, *sake*'s intoxicating character is of little relevance. Drinking *sake* does not necessarily mean being intoxicated in the sense of getting falling-down drunk. Alcoholic spirits are, after all, linked with spirituality in other religious traditions as well without necessarily entailing drinking to the state of inebriation. The Christian Eucharist, for example, often includes the use of wine as part of its sacramental celebration of Christian community. Wine serves a similar function in certain Jewish rituals.

Yet *sake*'s intoxicating qualities should not be ignored. The consumption of alcohol in Japan—and historically this has meant *sake*—has played an important role in Japanese social negotiations throughout history. Japanese (males especially) are noted for drinking alcohol as a release from the country's rigorous social norms. In the workplace, the Japanese hierarchical system places heavy demands on individual behavior. One is expected always to defer to superiors and to attend to the needs of subordinates. During after-hours drinking with one's coworkers, however, the strict social rules tend to evaporate. Stories are legion of intoxicated lower or mid-level managers in Japan who directed highly critical comments to their superiors only to be forgiven the next morning when their apology was accompanied by a reference to having drunk too much. Psychologists, anthropologists, and sociologists have commonly analyzed Japanese drinking as a safety valve for releasing pent-up pressures from restrained anger left over from the rigid daily routine.

Furthermore, communal drinking is a form of bonding found in many cultures. The German sense of gemütlichkeit, for example, is nowhere stronger than in beer halls. When two Germans formally celebrate the transition from using the polite *Sie* to the familiar *Du* form of address toward each other, it is traditionally celebrated with a toast of beer amidst interlocked arms. Communal drinking may dissolve the social walls between people, allowing them to discover their more intimate overlaps. *Sake*'s prominence in Shinto ritual cannot be fully understood without taking this function into account.

Of course, it is not always easy to distinguish when drinking *sake* is ritualistic and when it is simply the most direct route to getting drunk. When it comes to second nature, people seldom have a clear reason in mind for doing what they do. The spiritual values we have been discussing in this chapter are second nature to most Japanese. That is: since they are acculturated through repetition and tradition with little explanation, they get buried below the ordinary levels of self-reflective consciousness. Therefore, for some behavior, it is as difficult for Japanese to articulate true motivations as it would be for an outsider to surmise them. In sorting out the cultural significance of *sake* in Japanese culture today, a recent shift in Japanese drinking habits may give us a clue, however. Beer has replaced *sake* as Japan's most popular alcoholic beverage, and whiskey is finding its own niche as well. This includes drinks taken with meals. Even when about to partake in a traditional Japanese meal, the guest of honor is usually asked "beer or *sake?*" This phenomenon suggests *sake* might have lost its privileged status in everyday life.

Or has it? Many Japanese insist that beer should not be drunk while actually eating rice at a meal. When asked why, the most common answer is that "you will get sick." I know of no physiological basis for such a claim. People in other cultures commonly mix the two. Yet this does not mean the claim is untrue for *Japanese.* There may be psychosomatic forces at work. If *sake* and rice have the complex associations discussed in this chapter, it is possible they still function, perhaps on an unconscious level, with "being traditional" in Japan. Even though no longer the alcoholic beverage of choice, *sake* maintains its special associations within the Japanese value system. Perhaps rice and *sake* together function as a kind of cultural, if not Shinto, holographic entry point into "feeling traditional." If so, perhaps it seems wrong or unfitting that such an entry point should be adulterated with a "foreign" element like beer. Breaking a taboo (or fear of breaking a taboo) can make a person feel queasy. This psychological interpretation of the continuing status of *sake* is, of course, highly speculative. But we should not underestimate the way traditions become second nature and how the open violation of them can have an uncomfortable visceral effect for the person who grew up in that tradition.

In discussing Shinto values inherent in everyday Japanese affairs, we have thus far analyzed what we have called the "second-nature" level of cultural assimilation. These ideas, values, and practices are so embedded in Japanese tradition that they are seldom reflected upon or given an explicit rationale. Children learn them as part of the process of growing up—learning how to think, feel, and behave by modeling themselves after their elders. By examining the Japanese culture of rice, we were able to see how many of these Shinto values come to bear on the most ordinary affairs of daily life. In general we could say that, in much of what we have discussed up to now in this chapter, many Japanese are connected with Shinto in ways they themselves may not even immediately recognize. Of course, this is not the whole story. In the ebb and flow of life, most Japanese do sometimes think, feel, or behave in a way they themselves might label as "being Shinto."

Shinto Practices in Japanese Life

To appreciate the context of everyday Shinto-related behavior, it might be helpful to consider first a parallel situation from a Christian context in the West. Many Christians do not think much about their Christian identities in the course of their daily affairs. Suppose, however, we scrutinized these affairs as we have just examined those from the Japanese Shinto context. We could probably unearth a host of second-nature thoughts, feelings, and behavior reflecting Christian ideas or values such as guilt, forgiveness, charity, and hope. Most of these ideas would function so automatically that the people in question might only recognize their Christian roots if they explicitly looked for them. We could say the Christian inhabits a world of Christian habits. Yet such Christians may also, for example, regularly attend church services on Sundays. We could say this too is a Christianity-related habit, but there is a difference from the second-nature habits we have been discussing. On Sundays their going to church is intentional. They decide how to dress for church, think about whom they might meet there, and are generally aware that all these anticipated experiences will occur in a decidedly Christian context. If their Christian commitments are deeply spiritual, they may understand their church attendance as "practicing their Christianity." Even if this is not the case, the churchgoers would still see the behavior as "Christian" by association.

Returning to Shinto, let us now consider common practices in Japan that are analogous to our churchgoing example from Christianity. That is: let us examine experiences that may be habitual but involve a more self-conscious mentality than the second-nature behavior we have been analyzing. For some Japanese, such experiences may cluster around a strong self-identity with being Shinto. In other words: they might be seen as a religious practice central to their spirituality. For others, however, these same activities may be done more out of a sense of tradition, of preserving the continuity of family practices across the generations, or of meeting social expectations in a pro forma manner. For both groups of Japanese, it is important to note, they enter into such activities with awareness that their actions are connected in some way with Shinto. So let us call these "identifiably Shinto practices." We can group these practices into three categories: those related to Shinto senses of time, place, and instrumentality. As a general rule, we will focus on common practices familiar to most Japanese and that have relevance throughout the country, not just to one particular region or another. We begin with practices having a strong sense of timeliness.

TIMES TO BE SHINTO

Like most other religious traditions, Shinto celebrates the passage of time in two major respects: the biographical time marking the stages of a person's life and the calendrical time measuring the cycles of the year. Some religions—most notably the Abrahamic traditions of Judaism, Christianity, and Islam—find profound significance in a third kind of sacred time as well: the historical. For the most part, this sense of the sacred as working itself out through the events of religious history is not highlighted in Shinto. In celebrating passage through the stages of life, Shinto praxis tends to focus primarily on occasions related to human fertility and family—namely, birth, childhood, and marriage. From a knowledge of other religious traditions, one might expect Shinto to place special emphasis on the time of death, too, but it generally does not. We have already noted the Shinto taboo about contact with the dead, and in later chapters we will see why funerals in Japan tend to fall under the purview of Buddhism instead of Shinto.

Let us start, then, with the first stage of life: birth. About one month after birth, the newborn is brought to the Shinto shrine to be presented to the *kami*. The child has survived the trials of birth and has now lived long enough to be considered a new person in the local community. This rite is called the "first shrine visit." In ancient times this was probably a ritual to recognize the internal connection between the newborn and the tutelary *kami* protecting the village or clan. The hope would be that the *tama* in this shared relation would secure the health and safety of the child. According to the old ways, as we have seen, the mother—polluted by her blood spilled in childbirth—was not allowed to attend, but this prohibition is disappearing in practice if not in formal doctrine. Furthermore, with the displacement of the population to urban centers, the connection to the old homestead shrines has diminished to the point that a high percentage of these rituals are now performed at the larger, prestigious shrines instead of local ones.

The first shrine visit remains an important family event, however, and an occasion for dressing up and celebrating afterward.

The second stage of life is recognized in a ritual called "seven-five-three." This rite is celebrated in mid-November during the year in which the boy reaches the age of five or the girl either seven or three. In this ritual celebrating the transition from infancy to childhood, the children are dressed, often quite lavishly, in either kimono or *hakama* (skirted trousers). Originally the ritual may have signified the time when the child would begin to assume family duties of some sort, but this meaning is now probably forgotten. The significance of the particular ages of three, five, and seven may well derive from Chinese folk and Daoist traditions designating these ages as particularly susceptible to danger or the effect of malevolent forces.

The third life stage commonly recognized in formal Shinto ritual is marriage. When a marriage ceremony today includes religious rather than just secular components, the Shinto style of wedding is most common. (There are Buddhist and Christian-style weddings, too, sometimes even combinations wherein the bride and groom do a quick costume change between the traditional Japanese and Western wedding garb. When the format of a Christian wedding is followed in such cases, incidentally, it is usually more a fashion statement than the expression of any religious conviction.) In today's traditional wedding a Shinto priest typically presides, and a central part of the ceremony is the couple's drinking a series of small cups of *sake*. Although the Shinto ceremony seems to have become popular only during the last century, Shinto's combined emphasis on purity and fertility makes it particularly adaptable to the celebration of the marriage event.

The second group of Shinto practices marking the passage of time relates to annual cycles. New Year rituals are undoubtedly the most widely celebrated across Japan. The New Year is celebrated more as a season than a single day in Japan, and during the first week in January people traditionally make their ritualized "first visit" to a Shinto shrine (increasingly to the large ones with national prominence instead of the small local ones). Many Japanese make their "first visit" to a Buddhist temple in addition to—or even instead of—a Shinto shrine. Participants at the Shinto shrines often partake of special foods and imbibe the New Year *sake* after they have first been offered to the *kami*.

The *tama* arising from contact with the *kami* is thereby shared among the participants. In this New Year first shrine visit, there is the idea of purifying any defilements left over from the previous year and getting a fresh start on the new one. There are many local variations in the New Year rituals. At Yasaka shrine in Kyoto, for example, the priests light a sacred fire and people take home a punk lit from the fire to ignite the flame for cooking their first New Year meal.

Other rituals focus on various other key points in the annual cycle: time of planting, time of harvest, time of the solstice or equinox, and so forth. These points are usually celebrated in regional festivals along with other events germane to the locale. Generally these festivals are called *"matsuri"* and can vary in size from something not much more than a block party to events bringing millions of visitors from all over Japan and taking many months to prepare. In understanding the purpose of *matsuri*, it is useful to bear in mind that the term (meaning "enshrinement" or "elevation" or "deification") is linked with the term *"matsurigoto,"* which suggests government or administration. Hence at the heart of *matsuri* is the internal relation between the religious and the sociopolitical. Many *matsuri* celebrated today are not directly related to Shinto, but most of the older ones are. Thus on one level there is a religious event paying homage to a *kami* of local importance and on another level there is the community cooperation one might associate with a county fair. Although these levels may seem to run at cross-purposes, in practice they do not. The carnival (such as Mardi Gras) has served a similar function in European-derived cultures, for example.

Furthermore, the exuberance displayed in most *matsuri* harks back to the ancient myths of the celestial *kami*. In the next chapter we will see how celestial *kami* coaxed the sun *kami* out of her cave by having a raucous celebration that was certain to pique her curiosity. The story suggests that celestial *kami* enjoy a good time. Rather than insisting on acts of reverential kowtowing, they often seem to prefer a party given in their honor. One might say the *kami* want to be honored by being included in the festivities of life—which underscores Shinto spirituality as discovering and reflecting connectedness. Not only are people incomplete without the *kami;* the *kami* are incomplete without people.

In chapter 1 we compared the businessman's shrine visit to stopping by a friend's house for a chat without having any specific agenda in mind. The festive aspect of a *matsuri* can be compared to throwing a birthday party for that friend. The party brings together the guest of honor's friends and family so they can celebrate their interconnectedness with him. Even though some invitees to the party may not know each other, the gathering helps them discover how they are connected through their mutual friend. It is as if the party for the guest of honor becomes a holographic entry point for all the people to see and celebrate their interrelatedness. The *matsuri* functions in a similar way. On the social level, the festivities bring people together to celebrate their commonality. The *matsuri* participants sense their perhaps unknown

The Torii *at Miyajima*
One of the most famous torii *in Japan, this vermilion gate stands in the bay as an entrance to the Itsukushima shrine near Hiroshima.*

but assumed connectedness. On the religious level, it is an entry point for highlighting the people's intrinsic inseparability from the *kami* and at least potentially evokes the sense of living within a *kami*-filled, *tama*-energized world.

PLACES TO BE SHINTO

Through the centuries, various locales in Japan have acquired the reputation for being sites of extraordinary spiritual presence. As explained in the preceding chapter, according to general Shinto theory the entire world is infused with spiritual power, but there are places that for some reason seem to be more manifestly so. These become the holographic entry points for pilgrims. Many such sites— Mount Fuji, Ise, Miyajima, and so forth—are places of extraordinary beauty undisturbed by urban sprawl. Indeed their awe-inspiring beauty is part of their character as *kami* and what makes them stand out as parts-that-contain-the-whole. Because of the intimate connection between Shinto and nature, a visit to a famous mountain forest shrine may resemble a tourist stop at a national park. Interpretations of this confluence between Shinto pilgrimage and low-level eco-tourism often go along the following lines:

> The Japanese have become so secularized that these visits to remote shrines are devoid of spiritual significance. The people are just getting away from the cities for awhile to admire nature and enjoy some of the natural beauty for which parts of Japan are justly famous. Therefore, there is nothing particularly "religious" happening here at all. It is just a leisure activity and perhaps a chance to spend a little quality time with your family.

Building on our analysis from chapter 1, however, we can formulate a different explanation for the same behavior. The Japanese are not "getting away" but "going back." They are not there to "admire" nature but to "commune" with it. They are not "enjoying" natural beauty but allowing themselves to "be struck by it." It is not a "leisure activity" but a tranquil sense of "feeling at home." These subtle shifts in diction describe outwardly the same behavior, but they communicate a very different affect expressing many of the primary values we have been associating with Shinto. It is misguided to think that where there is no solemnity, no restraint, no explicit reverence toward a transcendent reality, there can be no religion. To insist on such a limited understanding of religion is to run the risk of missing many crucial elements of Shinto spirituality.

Furthermore, if only on a subliminal level, the *torii,* graveled areas, and *shimenawa* on the grounds remind visitors that these natural wonders can be portals into something more than objects for sightseeing. They can be the entry points into an intimate connectedness with all things. In this regard the account cited earlier was right to speak of the outing as "quality time with your family." But this "family" may be expanded to include all your intimate relations, not just the folks accompanying you on the train trip to the shrine.

Shinto sacred sites need not be limited to natural wonders, of course. As explained earlier, awe-inspiring natural objects are just one of many kinds of *kami.* There are shrines dedicated to deceased warriors, emperors, shoguns, scholars, and artists, for example. In urban areas the little neighborhood shrine or the grand complex of a place like the Meiji shrine in Tokyo can have the same effect as a shrine situated for its natural wonders. Furthermore many shrines, both urban and rural, both large and small, serve as annual sites for *matsuri* of their own—thereby coalescing sacred time and sacred place.

INSTRUMENTS FOR BEING SHINTO

Although scholars sometimes stress the separation between the sacred and the secular, most people live their daily lives by fluidly moving between the two. In times of joy or crisis, peace or stress, for example, people often feel the desire to be in touch with family and friends. So too do many Japanese feel a similar desire at such times to be in touch with *kami.* Here we will consider three practical ways Japanese ordinarily do so: through the use of amulets, through various petitions to the *kami,* and through distinctive prayer incantations called *norito.*

A major source of daily revenue at Shinto shrines, as at Buddhist temples, is in the selling of amulets. Each amulet or talisman is for a specific purpose. If, for example, you wish safe travel in vehicular traffic, you can purchase the amulet and hang it somewhere in your car. The comparable Roman Catholic item would be a St. Christopher medal. There are other amulets for purposes of health, doing well on exams, a favorable childbirth, good fortune in business, and so forth. They may be a small brocade bag with a drawstring or a small piece of wood or paper encased in a white paper wrapper tied with string. In either case, usually inscribed is the name of the shrine (or *kami*) and the benefit for which the charm is intended.

The practice of amulets is so ancient and widespread globally that its origin and rationale are difficult to identify. Anthropologists and religion scholars have various theories, many revolving around a belief in a metaphysical system linked to magic and sorcery. These explanations may assist in trying to understand origins, but they are less persuasive when we consider modern Shinto users of amulets or, for that matter, modern Roman Catholic users of St. Christopher medals. Perhaps, especially for contemporary practices, we need to supplement these theories with a psychological dimension: amulets and charms *remind* people of the sacred dimension of reality. From this standpoint, both the Catholic St. Christopher medal and the Shinto amulet for traffic safety serve as reminders to travelers that they never travel alone.

Let us try to translate this point into the terminology we have developed for discussing Shinto. The amulet is a kind of holographic entry point in its own right. By purchasing it and treating it with respect, one is reminded that one is part of a greater whole—a whole not beyond oneself but reflected *within* oneself. The amulet preserves one's conscious connection to the world as *kami*-filled and *tama*-powered. In this interpretation, at least for the modern context, the amulet is not the object of belief: it is a *reminder* of what one already believes but which, in the buzzing of everyday life, is likely to be forgotten. It is not all that different from the professional person's family photograph kept on the desk at work.

Another Shinto practice, closely related to the use of amulets, is the making of formal petitions to the *kami* by writing a request (or buying a prepackaged plea) on a small wooden plaque suspended on a special rack at the shrine. Sometimes these plaques are also used to give thanks for good fortune. In the same vicinity as the plaques, one often sees trees or bushes covered with little strips of folded paper. These too have a talismanic quality. At larger shrines, visitors may purchase small strips of paper on which they can read their fortune. The person then folds the strip of paper and attaches it to a tree branch or a string stretched between poles for this purpose. Most people just do it without rationale. But according to many, if you fold the fortune strip and leave it behind in that way, the fortune comes true. About as many people seem to think the opposite, however: by folding and attaching the strip, you prevent the fortune from coming true. The compromise position commonly heard in the shrines is that folding the paper around the tree branch will do both: if the slip of paper predicts good fortune, it will come true; if bad fortune, it will be prevented. Whatever the rationale, in many shrines one will find an area with dozens or even hundreds of such hanging fortune strips. Paper has other ritualistic functions in Shinto as well—partly because the ordinary Japanese word for "paper" is a homonym for *"kami."* In Shinto shrines one can often see paper folded into a zigzag pattern strung along a rope. Often they hang off *shimenawa* around sacred trees or rocks or

Votive Plaques
Visitors to Shinto shrines often write petitions to the kami *on wooden plaques and then hang the plaques on a stand in front of the shrine.*

connected to *torii*. They also form part of the wand made of branches
from a *sakaki* tree that the Shinto priest uses to purify a space.

Our final example of identifiably Shinto practices is that of *norito:*
incantations or prayers used at many Shinto occasions. The etymology of the term *"norito"* is obscure and somewhat controversial, but
a common interpretation holds that the word derives from roots suggesting speech "coming down from above" *(nori)* and "incantation"
(to). Given this derivation, the assumption is that the term originally
suggested the oracular speech by which the *kami* communicated to
people through a medium. In any case, for at least the past thousand
years or so *norito* have been understood to be fixed utterances used by
Shinto priests in performing certain rituals such as a New Year's blessing, a petition for a good harvest, or a blessing for a new house. The
earliest *norito* probably go back to preliterate times and were later
recorded in ancient texts like *Kojiki* (early eighth century). The formulas used today date mainly from a ritualistic text dating from the tenth
century called *Procedures of the Engi Period (Engishiki)*, but certainly
many were part of an oral tradition much earlier than this. Although
some *norito* are in Chinese (but using a Japanized pronunciation), the
bulk are in ancient Japanese. There are sections of *norito* where the
sonorous aspect seems more important than the content, suggesting
the potency in the words as voiced. This potency is probably related
to the notion of *kotodama*, the *tama* of words discussed in chapter 1.

Although the precise meanings of the *norito* incantations are sometimes uncertain, generally the prayers include snippets of details about
the *kami* to whom the norito is addressed. It seems likely that *norito*
were used in antiquity to appease the *kami* as part of a request for a
favor: purification, health, relief or protection from natural disaster,
and so forth. Citing the information about the *kami* may be a way of
proving that the supplicant already knows the *kami* and is building
on the internal relation between them. The details about the *kami*
included in the *norito* suggest the human has intimate knowledge of
the particular *kami* (and presumably vice versa). Therefore the modality of the *norito* is not simply to curry favor with *kami* or to use magic
to force them to do something for people. Rather, the *norito* confirms
an already existent relation—an overlap between *kami* and humans
—as a basis for future interaction.

EXISTENTIAL SHINTO SPIRITUALITY AND
EVERYDAY JAPANESE CULTURE

This chapter has shown how Shinto themes, values, and ideas touch the everyday lives of most Japanese people on two levels. Sometimes they function almost unconsciously as acculturated second nature. On the self-conscious level, there are regular occasions when most Japanese enter willingly into a decidedly Shinto context such as visiting a shrine, purchasing an amulet, or partaking in New Year's rituals. On both levels we have found continuities with the kinds of experiences discussed in chapter 1. This is possible in part because Shinto, at least as we have described it thus far, does not make a sharp dichotomy between the sacred and the secular. Because of the paradigm of the holographic entry point, the everyday particulars and the sacred whole are always reflected in each other.

If we grant that nine out of ten Japanese today, at least in some contexts, identify themselves as being "Shinto," they must be referring to an existential rather than essentialist form of Shinto spirituality. This spirituality allows them to feel connected with nature, with other people, and with a wondrous, awe-inspiring presence. Yet it does not exclude them from having other kinds of personal identity —even, for example, a Buddhist identity—that may be just as, or even more, important to them. Their existential Shinto spirituality can *describe* them without defining them. By labeling themselves as "Shinto," they can express something profound about the patterns followed in their lives without accepting that they should or must behave in that way. For them, therefore, the term "Shinto" describes more than it prescribes. This is part of the explanation for why the same Japanese who identify themselves as Shinto will say they do not have a religion *(shūkyō)*. As we have seen, the Japanese term *"shūkyō"* has nuances of essentialist qualities such as a prescriptive doctrinal system and sectarian exclusivity. Thus the term does not fit their sense of how Shinto operates in their own lives. Their existential Shinto spirituality may be an intimate concern without being an ultimate concern. They may derive profound meaning and a sense of spiritual connectedness from Shinto without necessarily making a metaphysical claim that Shinto's essence is at the inviolate core of their being.

All this is not to suggest that an essentialist Shinto spirituality is impossible or even extremely rare in Japan. For some Japanese, Shinto is undoubtedly a defining feature in who and what they understand themselves to be. For these essentialists, Shinto values are to be nurtured through rigorous praxis, Shinto ideas to be studied in systematic doctrinal ways, and Shinto institutions to be supported enthusiastically. For them to do anything less would be hypocritical, a form of insincerity by which they present themselves to be other than what they really are. For some, such an essentialist identity would preclude any participation in Buddhist activities, since this would defile the purity of the mindful heart. For others, a pro forma participation might be allowed as a concession to social harmony; but however much those practices might be Buddhist, one's identity as a "Buddhist" can only be existential. Essentially one would still be Shinto.

When evaluating Shinto existential and essentialist spiritualities, there may be a temptation to say that one is genuine and the other a distortion or that one is traditional and the other new. Such an evaluation is superficial. It shows a lack of understanding about the complex dynamic between these two forms of Shinto spirituality that has evolved through the expanse of Japanese history. Furthermore, there may be readers who know something of Japanese culture and are cynical about the analysis presented in this book so far. They might accuse my account of romanticizing Shinto into some pure religious spirituality, Zen-like in its qualities of responsiveness and openness. They might reasonably ask what this analysis has to do with divine emperors and kamikaze pilots, with imperialist expansion and militarism, or with the Shinto-based ideologies claiming Japanese ethnic, racial, and national superiority. To address these issues we must look more closely into the evolution of Shinto in Japanese history. Hence our concerns in the next three chapters will be historical.

CHAPTER 3

Ancient Shinto (Prehistory—794)
The Trailblazers

The first chapter began with the experience of Shinto spirituality in its most general, not even necessarily Japanese, form. Chapter 2 described contemporary Japanese cultural behavior laden with the underlying values and ideas associated with this experience and the Shinto heritage as it has come to be part of the daily lives of many Japanese today. The next three chapters focus on the historical development of Shinto from prehistoric times up to the present—giving special attention to Shinto institutional, doctrinal, and political structures. Surveying this extensive period, we will find throughout elements of both existential and essentialist Shinto. But we will also find a historical dynamic between them that developed in three major phases. This chapter considers the earliest phase of Shinto spirituality: from prehistory up to around the end of the eighth century. Here we will find the foundations for both existential and essentialist modalities. Chapter 4 continues the narrative from 794 up to 1801, the year in which Motoori Norinaga died. As we will see, elements of existential Shinto spirituality tended to flourish during that millennium. Chapter 5 covers the last two centuries of the story—1801 through 2002—describing the rise and ultimate dominance of essentialist over existential characteristics during the war years and then the awkward tension between the two continuing up to the present. To understand the relation between Shinto as folk religion and state religion, between Shinto as a form of personal spirituality and as a nationalist ideology, between Shinto as a religious organization and civil institution, it is crucial to grasp the impact and distinctiveness of each of these three historical phases. To begin our story, let us consider the account of Shinto most often found in reference books dealing with either Japan or comparative religion.

The "Standard" Account of Shinto

Relying on preconceived notions about religion, Western commentators have often molded their narratives of Shinto into a form convenient and digestible for their Western audience. Extrapolating from the religions in their own cultures, Westerners often look in other religions for a scriptural foundation and narratives about gods creating the world. Using this template, standard descriptions of Shinto often include a summary statement something like this:

> Shinto is an animistic Japanese religion going back to preliterate times. The myths of creation and how the state was established were preserved in oral traditions until written down in the early eighth century in two chronicles, *Kojiki* and *Nihonshoki*. These chronicles narrate the beginning of the gods and goddesses *(kami)* and the process by which the islands of Japan (or by extension the whole world) came into being through their actions. The most important deity is the Sun Goddess, Amaterasu. She is considered the direct ancestor of the Japanese imperial family and gives the throne a religious foundation.

Such explanations appear in dozens of Western books and reference works dealing with Japan. Since, as we will see, they support an essentialist interpretation of Shinto, they commonly appear in nineteenth- and twentieth-century Japanese accounts as well—the same era when modern Western scholarship first turned its attention to Japan. If we were to go back two or three centuries earlier, however, most Japanese of the time would fail to recognize in the description their own version of "Shinto" spirituality. So, despite its claims, the standard account is not so traditional at all. It is a distinctively nineteenth- and twentieth-century reading of what is most fundamental to Shinto. How such a narrative became authoritative will be explained in chapter 5. Even at this point in our study, though, we can see in this standard account two emphases that do not match the descriptions in chapters 1 and 2.

First, there is at least the indirect suggestion that Shinto is a text-based religion comparable to Judaism, Christianity, Islam, or even Confucianism in that it is a "religion of the book." This leads people to think of *Kojiki* or *Nihonshoki* as scriptures or foundational sacred texts of Shinto. If this were true, we might expect Japanese to commonly read the texts or at least have parts of them memorized. Phrases from the works would permeate the idioms of the culture (as one finds hundreds of phrases like "turn the other cheek" in cultures influenced by the Christian Bible, for example). Yet this is hardly the case. Furthermore, given the hierarchy of the *kami* mentioned in the texts, one might assume that Shinto shrines were built with the same hierarchy of deities in mind. But for the most part they were not. Most Shinto shrines in Japan, especially the small ones found in neighborhoods and villages, have little relation to the major *kami* upon which the two chronicles focus.

The second oddity is that the standard account takes the term *"kami"* to refer primarily to the celestial "gods" and "goddesses" of the creation narratives. Yet our analyses have shown the meaning of *kami* to be much broader than this, including almost anything that is awe-inspiring. That is: from the standpoint of general Shinto practice and belief, the personal deities of creation are only one kind of *kami*. For reasons that will become clear in our ensuing discussion of Shinto's development, though, essentialist Shinto tends to emphasize the deities of creation as the paradigm for *kami*. Given the essentialist Shinto's standard narrative, an unsuspecting reader might assume that Shinto is a polytheistic religion with a fixed hierarchy of personal deities much like those of ancient Greece or Rome. In Greco-Roman polytheism, however, it was critical to know which deity was which and where each was worshiped. It would be dangerous—even life threatening as Homeric tales explain—not to know which heavenly deity was associated with one's present situation. The ancient Greeks often found themselves as pawns in rivalries and conflicts among the deities, whereas this kind of abuse of humans by the celestial *kami* is rare in either Shinto myths or people's interpretation of ordinary events. The Shinto world is indeed filled with vengeful spirits, goblins, changelings, and tutelary deities. But ancient Shinto did not understand the human world as a toy for divine amusement or as ego extensions of divine personalities. Although divine rivalries do appear in the stories of *Kojiki* and *Nihonshoki,* they were played out for the most part on the celestial plane, not through manipulation of the human realm.

The narratives of supernatural deities did, however, serve well the ideologies of both Japan and its Western adversaries in the nineteenth and twentieth centuries. On the one hand, it was reassuring for the militarist Japanese to think that celestial deities of cosmic import were going to protect the empire with supernatural intervention. For Japan's Western enemies, on the other hand, the interpretation of "*kami*" as "deity" helped inspire monotheistic soldiers to go off to war against heathens who believed their emperor to be a god. Given such political ramifications, it is easy to see why the standard narrative would gain so much currency on both sides of the Pacific in the nineteenth and twentieth centuries.

In this chapter we will deconstruct the standard narrative by focusing on what it omits and investigating the historical reasons modern scholars—both Western and Japanese—might have consciously or unconsciously marginalized or overlooked such material. First we will look at ancient sources of Shinto outside the textual tradition of *Nihonshoki* and *Kojiki*. Free of biases about sacred texts and celestial deities, we will discover other elements influencing ancient Shinto spirituality. Second we will look more closely at the history of *Nihonshoki* and *Kojiki* as texts. Why were they written? Why does the standard account so often blur the differences between the two? What in *Kojiki* especially enabled its meteoric rise from relative obscurity to becoming a cornerstone for a new image of the Japanese state in the nineteenth century?

Alternative Sources

To address this issue, we must go back to preliterate times, that is, to Japan before the fifth or sixth century. The evidence is sparse. We have some archaeological data, some modern anthropologically accessible practices suggestive of patterns that might have originated in this early period, and a smattering of cryptic accounts by Chinese visitors to the Japan of that time. From this evidence most scholars speculate that the ancient Japanese were animists—that is, believers in spirits who operate in both the natural and human domains. To ward off bad spirits and invite good spirits, they used amulets. Communicating with the spirits probably followed shamanistic forms related to those of Siberia and Korea. (There are also linguistic reasons for connecting

Japan with these mainland areas.) Archaeological digs have discovered prehistoric settlements throughout the Japanese archipelago suggestive of clanlike groups called *uji*. Each *uji* probably had its own special guardian *kami (ujigami)*. In the Japanese stone age (up to about 300 B.C.E.), hunter-gatherer groups lived in caves and pits on the hillsides.

By the Yayoi period (300 B.C.E. to 300 C.E.), most Japanese had settled in the plains where they formed communities dedicated to wet rice culture, fishing, and vegetable gardening. For these enterprises, it was advantageous for people to cooperate on the village level. Judging from archaeological evidence of differentiated burial practices within these communities, the sedentary *uji* probably had hierarchical social orders, with the leaders enjoying both religious and political power (hence the close relation between *matsuri* and *matsurigoto* mentioned in chapter 2). Reverence for the *ujigami* undoubtedly carried over into this new social structure. It is likely, for example, that the sun *kami* Amaterasu was originally the *ujigami* of the Yamato, the *uji* that became the Japanese imperial family. With the Yamato rise to power, the status of their tribal deity ascended with them. Such a sense of *kami* informs *Kojiki* and *Nihonshoki:* the celestial *kami* in the creation narratives likely derived from the early *ujigami;* their hierarchies in the texts probably reflect the relative power of the *uji* from which they sprang.

Besides the *ujigami,* the notion of *kami* had at least two other associations in the preliterate period: the awe-inspiring aspects of nature and the spirits of the dead. The geography of Japan helps explain this prehistoric religious veneration of the natural world. In broad terms, the physical setting of Japan is benign. The islands are subtropical in the south and temperate in the north with quite constant patterns of seasonal rain and predictable growing seasons. Arable land is not extensive, but what there is, mostly lava-derived soil, lends itself well to certain kinds of farming. The sea provides an abundant supply of fish and seaweed. Still, nature is capricious in Japan. As mentioned in chapter 2, Japan is still a geologically young volcanic archipelago— making the country unusually susceptible to devastating earthquakes, volcanic activity, landslides, and flash floods. And its southwest-to-northeast axis leaves Japan vulnerable to the full brunt of typhoons.

Consequently, although the environment is generally conducive to sustenance, disaster can occur at almost any time. In such a context, the prehistoric Japanese people likely believed in capricious forces needing appeasement—and this, in turn, probably led to rites directed to the nature-related *kami*. This might also explain the large number of talismanic figurines found in archaeological digs.

Furthermore, as the large game disappeared from the forests, people abandoned the mountains and began to settle in the small plains within the valleys where the soil was conducive to farming. The farmers became increasingly estranged from the mountain forests. With their majestic waterfalls, towering trees, strange rocks, foxes, and badgers, these wildernesses became not only the sites of folklore but also holographic focal points for connecting with the mysterious, awesome power of *kami*. We find this theme beautifully rendered even today in popular Japanese *anime* such as *Princess Mononoke*. As noted in the preceding chapter, a large number of shrines are in mountain and forest areas that people must travel far from the cities to visit.

The other primordial sense of *"kami"* was to refer to the spirits of the dead. One ancient view of the afterlife (as found in *Kojiki,* for example) held that after death people go to the dark underworld, the Land of Yomi. This was a Hades-like place where the dead—regardless of behavior in this world—went to rot for all time. This idea befits the death taboo discussed earlier. Given this bleak picture of the afterlife, it is not surprising that in later Japanese culture most ideas or rituals centering on death and its sequel derived from the imported religion of Buddhism, not the indigenous Shinto. For relatives and friends in preliterate Japan, it cannot have been very consoling to think of the deceased as residing permanently in Shinto's Land of Yomi. Buddhist doctrine, by contrast, introduced the notion of heavens and hells as a system of reward and punishment, as well as the general idea of rebirth. Buddhist rites guided the deceased in negotiating the transmigrations beginning after death. As time passed, Japanese funerary rites became increasingly a Buddhist domain.

The ancient Japanese view of afterlife is a little more complicated than this, however. Besides the Buddhist and the Land of Yomi representations, there is yet another strain still visible in various Japanese folk beliefs and practices, especially related to shamanism. This is the notion of a spirit world. If the shaman is to communicate with the dead, the spirits must obviously be available somewhere to be contacted. Folk belief holds that there is a ghostly realm interlaced with the world of humans. Under certain conditions, the spirits (called *tamashii* or simply *tama*) present themselves to and through the living. Folktales of vengeful spirits, ghostly monsters, and transformations between animals and spirits richly portray the interpenetration of the two realms. As expected when dealing with a tradition related to shamanism, this realm is accessed through trance or dream as well. Consequently, there are numerous legends of people's intentional and unintentional visits to the various domains of spirits, deities, heavenly beings, goblins, and ghosts.

Let us consider one example of an extant practice suggesting this ancient worldview. In the northeastern part of the main island of Honshu there is a mountain commonly known as "Osorezan"—literally "Fright Mountain." On summer evenings, pilgrims go there to visit the women shamans. It is a bizarre landscape of former lava flows, steam vents without much vegetation, and air pungent with brimstone. If one were going to meet the dead spirits someplace halfway between their world and ours, this would be as good a site as any. The shaman, blind by birth and trained in a discipline culminating in a ritual marriage with a *kami,* has the ability to communicate with the dead—to be a channel for the deceased to converse with their living loved ones.

It is tempting to think of such phenomena as long-held superstitions living out their remaining days before the ultimate victory of enlightened reason. One might suspect that well-educated Japanese do not think in terms of communing with the dead and that if they were to visit Osorezan, for example, it would be more like a trip an American might make to the sulfur pits of Yellowstone Park than a religious pilgrimage. Yet as we learned from chapter 2's discussion of family outings to mountain Shinto shrines, such an interpretation may be too facile. A pair of religion scholars—one a native Japanese and one an American—told me they had informally surveyed their students in Japan as to whether they ever "talked to their dead ancestors." In their informal sampling (at one of Japan's most prestigious national universities known for its studies in science and technology), over 90 percent said they did. A bit surprised by the result, they then asked the students if their dead ancestors ever replied. More than 75 percent said yes. Without further study in a statistically controlled context, it is difficult to know what to make of such a response. The point is that scientific education in modern Japan may not simply eliminate and supplant the ancient Japanese notion that interaction with the spirit realm is possible.

Of course, communicating with the dead may not take the literal form of the Osorezan encounters. The activity may be more a psychological or spiritual remembrance—a pattern commonly found in the annual Japanese festival of Obon. Obon is a nominally Buddhist celebration in midsummer that involves revering and communing with one's dead ancestors. It is "nominally Buddhist" because the festival is said to derive from a Chinese Buddhist text called in Japanese the *Urabon* (Sanskrit: *Ullambana*) *Sutra*. Despite the text's claim to be a translation of a Buddhist work from India, scholars have not found any evidence or mention of the alleged Sanskrit equivalent. Using purely Indian Buddhist assumptions, one would expect the dead ancestors to have most likely moved on, having been reborn into this or some other world, whether mundane, celestial, or infernal. So the text is hypothesized to be of Chinese origin. Presumably it was written as Buddhism's response to its new cultural context, where venerating ancestors had already been a firmly established tradition for many centuries. In any case the tradition took root in Japan and flourished.

As the tradition developed in Japan (going back at least to the seventh century), Obon is understood as a time for the living to party with their dead ancestors. Obon activities may include evening circle dances lit by lanterns and rhythmically performed to the beat of large drums. (Western moviegoers may recall the final scene in the popular Hollywood film *The Karate Kid II*.) Or families visit their ancestral family plots to picnic with the dead. Sometimes special rites of veneration are held in the home before the small household altar. One could argue whether Obon is really Buddhist, Shinto, Confucian, or folk tradition, but this would be missing the point. In this case at least, the traditions overlap in an internal relation. The Obon festival is about the living people's connections with their dead relatives, and in this ritualized behavior the denominational boundaries are not relevant. In the final analysis, if more than 90 percent of the living Japanese are

Shinto and over 70 percent are Buddhist, why should that change in the afterlife?

Besides the Obon evidence of the dead's continued engagement with this world, we also find from ancient times the Shinto practice of appeasing the vengeful spirits of powerful individuals who died under foul circumstances. To assuage spirits who might return in anguish to haunt the living, people often gave those spirits the formal status of *kami* and erected an appropriate shrine. Such shrines are not so much memorials to the greatness of the dead as they are amulets to ward off a dangerous spirit. They are for appeasing a presently existing spirit of the dead, not to pay tribute to the life of the deceased. When Emperor Kammu decided to move out of Nara and establish a new capital in the late eighth century, for instance, he first chose a site in a nearby region called Nagaokakyō. The move was rife with political schemes. An administrator could get rich and influential by controlling the permits for construction in the new capital. The ensuing intrigues resulted in the death of the aristocrat in charge, Fujiwara no Tanetsugu (735–785). This event was followed by the probable assassination of one of his alleged murderers, Prince Sawara, the emperor's brother. From this point on, everything concerning the new construction at Nagaokakyō seemed to go wrong and the blame fell on the vengeful spirits of Tanetsugu and Sawara. Emperor Kammu pulled up roots again and moved the capital to Heian (Kyoto). To cover his back, he had a shrine built to appease and pacify the vengeful spirits.

A Shinto shrine for pacifying the spirit of an angry ghost can sometimes evolve into a positive source of power as well. In Kyoto, for example, we find Kitano shrine, originally built to appease the spirit of Sugawara no Michizane (845–903). An aristocrat respected for his learned mastery of Chinese classics, Michizane found himself on the wrong side of a political maneuver and was banished to the southern island of Kyushu. There he is said to have developed powers of wizardry. After his death in exile, earthquakes and floods ravaged Kyoto, lending credence to the idea that Michizane's spirit was on a rampage. The court built the splendid Kitano shrine in Kyoto and another major shrine in his honor in Kyushu. The calamities came to an end. Posthumously elevated to the highest court rank, Michizane also received a deity's name: Temman Tenjin. In the ensuing centuries, he became a patron saint for literature, poetry, and calligraphy. Temman shrines sprouted up throughout Japan, and even today young Japanese go to his shrine to pray for help on exams.

In the cases of both Michizane and Tanetsugu/Sawara, the dead spirits are *kami*. Like *kami* in general, however, the *tama* of the dead spirits may be either beneficial or harmful to humans. Their enshrinement recognizes the awesome quality and potential power of the dead. Clearly the *tama*—whether beneficent or malevolent—can survive the physical death of the person. Exactly how to understand this phenomenon remains a problem within Shinto doctrine, and in chapter 5 we will examine one specific manifestation of its ambiguity—the current controversy around Yasukuni shrine in Tokyo.

To review: antedating the two chronicles' treatment of *kami* as celestial deities involved in creation, we find evidence of three other senses of *kami*. First, once Japan organized into settled communities there was formal recognition of *ujigami* as deities who specifically related to the political/religious leadership in the *uji*. These were the probable precursors to the celestial deities cited in *Kojiki* and *Nihonshoki*. Second, considering awe-inspiring natural phenomena to be *kami* seems to be a phenomenon going back to earliest times. Third, equally old is the idea of the spirits of the dead having an awesome power that can be managed by granting them *kami* veneration. With this expanded context for the origins of Shinto in mind, let us return to the texts that initiated this discussion: *Kojiki* (Record of ancient matters) and *Nihonshoki* (Chronicles of Japan).

The Relation Between Nihonshoki *and* Kojiki

The early eighth-century chronicles are often considered twin narratives. This association is understandable. Certainly both texts resulted from imperial directives to record the origins of Japan and trace the imperial ancestral line. Moreover, both *Kojiki* and *Nihonshoki* survey the time period from before the creation of Japan to their compilation in the early eighth century. Yet their emphases differ. *Kojiki* is rich in detail about the mythic preliterate period from the origins of Japan to the imperial rulers of the sixth century. In comparison, *Nihonshoki* has much more detail about the emperors from the sixth century up to the date of its writing. In this respect, the two narratives complement each other. Furthermore, on most points of overlap the two chronicles either agree or at least do not blatantly contradict one another. And, finally, both texts offer a mytho-historical justification for the Japanese imperial system: both trace the lineage of the emperors back to the celestial *kami* at the time of creation. Whatever their commonalities, however, the differences between the two texts are equally important for understanding Shinto spirituality and its institutional history. The most obvious difference is that the chroniclers wrote *Kojiki* mostly in Japanese, *Nihonshoki* totally in Chinese. This suggests different intended audiences.

The Chinese text of *Nihonshoki*—its narrative mode and literary style as well as the language itself—would be accessible to any elite, educated East Asian reader. Indeed it is modeled on the narrative style of Chinese dynastic histories. *Nihonshoki* was therefore suitable for presenting foreigners with an authoritative document about Japanese culture and its religio-political foundations. As such, the compilation of *Nihonshoki* was part of a larger international public relations campaign. In the Nara period (710–794) the Japanese court showcased for the world its aspirations as a major civilization. For the first time, the Japanese established a permanent metropolitan capital, modeling it on Chang'an, the capital of Tang China. Up to then, because of the death taboo and the fear of vengeful ghosts, the court had constructed a new imperial palace upon the death of each ruling monarch. To project itself as a major civilization, the Japanese court decided at the turn of the eighth century that it needed a grand capital city with a permanent palace, geometrically arranged boulevards, and massive religious monuments at the appropriate compass points. Nara was the site chosen for this enterprise. As part of this city plan, Emperor Shōmu constructed the Great Temple to the East (Tōdai-ji), the largest wooden structure in the world. (It still is, in fact, although its present version is somewhat smaller than the original.) Inside Tōdai-ji is the world's largest seated bronze Buddha (over fifty feet in height). When the temple opened, the emperor sent out invitations throughout the known extent of civilization. Gifts or emissaries arrived from as far away as Persia. In such a period of cultural public relations, it is understandable Japan would want a formal chronicle of its history befitting such cultural aspirations and accomplishments. *Nihonshoki* fit the bill.

Nihonshoki's scholarly methods and assumptions also befit its international audience. The research involved compiling the histories (written in Chinese) preserved in the treasure-houses of the various *uji*. The *Nihonshoki* chroniclers were less worried about having a consistent story than accounting for all the evidence. Thus they sometimes included variant accounts and, for topics like creation myths, would even draw on Chinese narratives as well. Such inclusiveness, the editors probably believed, would enhance mainlanders' appreciation not only of the text but also of the compilers' sophistication as historians.

Kojiki, by contrast, was not compiled to impress foreigners. It was written mainly in Japanese, a language just barely beginning to develop a written form of its own. Few people, even few Japanese, would be able to read it. It differed from *Nihonshoki* in its sources and historiographic method, too. *Kojiki* was supposedly compiled from Japanese oral traditions memorized by a court storyteller named Hieda no Are. The storyteller's task was to collect the various extant oral narratives and weave them together into a single coherent story. Then a scribe would write it all down. The final text would preserve not only the mytho-historical account but also some ancient Japanese *norito* and poems. In short, *Kojiki* was, at least in part, a cultural preservation project. Just as folklorists and ethnomusicologists today try to preserve oral traditions before they are lost forever, compiling *Kojiki* was a way to protect Japan's cultural heritage. *Kojiki* was meant for the Japanese themselves.

Kojiki's system of writing would be crucial to Shinto's later history. How to render spoken Japanese into written form remained a problem throughout the eighth century. Until the introduction of Chinese texts in the late fifth or early sixth century C.E., Japan had had no writing system at all. Because classical Chinese and ancient Japanese are fundamentally unrelated and dissimilar languages, though, the use of Chinese characters for writing in Japanese was, at best, awkward. It took some three centuries before the kind of Japanese writing system used today could develop. During the sixth and seventh centuries, Japanese simply wrote in Chinese, not Japanese. At the turn of the eighth century, however, the Japanese experimented with rendering Japanese into a hybrid writing system using Chinese characters—but not always in exactly the same ways as those characters had been used in China.

The precipitating cause for the experimentation was the court's hope to preserve in writing the ancient Japanese traditions that had up to then been either handed down orally in Japanese or translated into literary Chinese. Thus *Kojiki* became Japan's first book written in the country's native language. Because the experimentation in orthography was a continuing enterprise, though, the writing systems used in the eighth century often varied from text to text and sometimes even within texts. It was not until the ninth century that a version of the present writing system—which combines a syllabary (denoting only pronunciation) and Chinese characters (generally denoting meaning as well as pronunciation)—was developed. By the time the writing system was fully standardized, however, certain early eighth-century forms of Japanese orthography had become so antiquated and forgotten that significant parts of them were often unintelligible, even to the well educated.

Kojiki is an excellent example of how bizarre the old orthography could be. Most frustrating, the text's writing system is not even internally consistent. Some parts of *Kojiki* are in regular classical Chinese (like *Nihonshoki*). Other sections use Chinese characters as a syllabary—that is, the writers used the characters stripped of their Chinese meanings, retaining only the Chinese pronunciation as a rough approximation for a Japanese sound. At other points, whole Japanese words are expressed with a single Chinese character whose meaning seemed analogous. Adding still further confusion, some sections of *Kojiki* use hybrids of these options. The result: any Japanese wishing to read the whole *Kojiki* would have to decode, not simply read, the text. Ability to read other texts in Chinese and Japanese, even other texts from the eighth century, would not necessarily guarantee literacy with respect to *Kojiki*.

Because of its idiosyncratic writing system, its appearance in an era when admiration for things Chinese was still strong, and the availability of a comparable text written in readily accessible Chinese, *Kojiki* fell into relative obscurity until the eighteenth century. *Nihonshoki* became the more commonly cited authoritative account. After all, it was in the elite language of East Asian intellectuals (Chinese); it was much more detailed in treating events from recent Japanese history; its narrative had a scholarly or historical rather than mythological feel;

and it was sufficient for establishing the imperial lineage and the connection of that family to the celestial *kami*. There was probably also the assumption that on all crucial points it basically agreed with *Kojiki*. Having compared the language, the historiography, the audience, and the orthography of the two texts, let us now turn to their contents.

According to both ancient chronicles, the celestial *kami* lived in a heavenly field or plain predating the existence of human beings and even the earth as we know it. The *kami* deities themselves have a lineage. The accounts depict them as neither omnipotent nor omniscient. They have personalities much like human beings, including foibles as well as virtues. According to the ancient narratives, spats among the deities sometimes had an indirect adverse effect on the physical world. For example, the storm *kami*, Susanoo, liked to taunt his sister the sun *kami*, Amaterasu. The result at one point, as explained in *Kojiki*, is that Amaterasu retired into a cave to pout and, without the sun, the sky went dark. The rest of the *kami* deities plotted to get Amaterasu out of the cave. They put on a boisterous party outside her hideout, knowing that Amaterasu's love of a good time and general curiosity would cause her to peek outside. When she did, the deities used a mirror to cast back her own brilliant reflection. Concerned that there was another sun deity replacing her, Amaterasu came out of the cave, sparkling with envy, where she was captured and finally cajoled to stay outside. So, once again, there is "illumination in the heavens" (the literal meaning of Amaterasu's name).

It is noteworthy that Amaterasu's brother, Susanoo, is not an evil figure, however short-tempered and violent he might appear. As suggested by our earlier discussion of defilement and purification, even in the ancient myths Shinto does not generally emphasize a struggle between good and evil. Indeed Susanoo is more like a pesky, immature delinquent. He defecates in the middle of his sister's palace and then defiles it further with a skinned colt. Although a celestial *kami* can cause serious problems—Susanoo's shenanigans, after all, led to a world cast in darkness—the Shinto myths lack the cosmic struggle between good and evil found in many other religions. Furthermore, the relation between the celestial *kami* and humans is unlike that of certain traditions familiar from Western mythology. The celestial *kami* are not an order of being separate from humans; the two are part of a shared lineage. Thus a Japanese man like Michizane can become a *kami* whereas a Greek human was often punished for aspiring to be godlike. For Shinto, if the person has a pure mindful heart the *kami* is discovered within oneself. It is not that one individual (a human) establishes a relation with another individual (the *kami* deity). Instead the human enters the holographic focal point, the gateway to an awesome mystery that feels like home. It is home for an extended family of *kami* and humans sharing in a corporate *tama*. Although all humans ultimately trace back historically to the mysterious power of the celestial *kami* who created the world, it is easy to lose touch with this internal connectedness. With an undefiled *kokoro*, however, the human can pass through the gate to connectedness and experience the interlaced relation between *kami* and humans that has been there all along. This Shinto gateway leads, not to somewhere else (an Olympus or even the celestial plain of Japanese myth), but to where one has really been all along—in the spiritual whole as reflected in each of us. Such an understanding would be quite alien, for example, to Greek conceptions of divinity and humanity.

It is curious, too, that the celestial *kami* are more vulnerable than the immortal deities of ancient Greece. The ancient chronicles relate that Izanami is burned in giving birth to the Fire God, then dies and goes to the netherworld of the Land of Yomi to decompose. This event makes Izanami more like a Greek demigoddess than goddess—that is, although divine, she is susceptible to the same passing over into an afterlife as is a human. The suggestion is that the bifurcation between the divine and the human is not absolute in Shinto. Furthermore, the *kami* deities, like *kami* in general, are material as well as spiritual. They are not pure *tama*, lacking corporeality, but the more indivisibly material/spiritual form of *tama* as *mi* or *mono*. Amaterasu is not an invisible deity like Apollo, who rides a chariot pulling the sun across the sky. Amaterasu is the actual physical sun *itself.* The sun is a material/spiritual sacred reality. This brings us to the discussion of the emperor or empress as *kami*.

Justifying the Imperial System

Scholars often point out that the two chronicles, *Nihonshoki* and *Kojiki,* established a religious-philosophical justification for the sovereignty of the imperial family. We need to understand this statement in context, however. During the seventh and eighth centuries, three such justifications developed. Along with the Shinto-based rationale, there was also an explanation based in Confucianism and another in Buddhism. In fact, at least in terms of being expressed in written form, Shinto's was the last to be formally articulated. So let us begin with the two earlier, non-Shinto, arguments for the unique authority of the imperial family.

We find allusions to the Confucian justification in the language of Japan's first "constitution": the Seventeen-Article Constitution or, as it is often called, the Shōtoku Constitution, said to have been promulgated in 604. Written in Chinese (like all other texts in Japan at the time), the document sometimes uses Chinese Confucian terminology in its explanation of imperial rule: "heaven," "ritual appropriateness," "harmony," and "filial piety," for example. Because the Confucian justification for imperial rule in China would be well known to anyone who could read such a Chinese document, the full Confucian argument is more suggested than explicated. The general point of the Chinese Confucian theory was that the emperor or empress is directly tied to heaven and governs in accord with the heavenly way. This makes the sovereign a link between "what is above" (the celestial) and "what is below" (the earth and the people). The harmony of the state derives from the balanced integration of above and below: what is above is to care for those below; those below are to revere and be loyal to what is above. If everyone—sovereign and people alike—acts appropriately to their position, the state will prosper.

The Confucian state ideology did not enter unchanged into the Japanese context, however. Two differences are particularly noteworthy. First, in Confucian state ideology, if the emperor or empress does not reign as a monarch should, the empire will not accord with the harmonizing patterns of the heavens. Disorder will follow and the people are duty-bound to overthrow the inauthentic sovereign. There is not even a hint of this idea in the Japanese constitution, however, or in any other documents of the era. Thus the Japanese Seventeen-Article Constitution accepted the Chinese Confucian ideal of sovereignty selectively, not as whole cloth. A second difference is that the Japanese added something. Unlike the typical Chinese Confucian theory of the state, the Japanese constitution explicitly connected the harmony of the state with each official's psychological introspection. Officials were called on to explore their own personal motives in order to eliminate traces of egoism. This is a Buddhist influence. It is noteworthy that the second article of the Shōtoku Constitution gave Buddhism the status of a state religion and explicitly commanded the Japanese to revere the "Three Jewels": the Buddha, the Buddhist teachings, and the Buddhist community. Let us briefly consider, then, how Buddhism lent its own religious rationale for the Japanese imperial state.

The constitution was purportedly written under the aegis of Prince Regent Shōtoku who, like his aunt Empress Suiko and most other members of the Soga family, was a devout Buddhist. It is significant that Shōtoku is also associated with a commentary on the Indian Buddhist *Sutra of Queen Śrīmālā* (Japanese: *Shōmangyō*). Queen Śrīmālā was a female Indian monarch (as Suiko was a female Japanese monarch) who exemplified both Buddhist enlightenment and compassion in her rulership. As monarch of a Buddhist state, she abided by its ideals of compassion and fairness to all classes. In emphasizing this text, Shōtoku was obviously drawing parallels with the benign rulership of his aunt, the Japanese empress. This brings us back to the issue of Buddhist introspection. Buddhism introduced to Japanese culture an appreciation for the function of states of mind, behavioral habits, and deep-rooted psychological motivations. The Buddhist system of self-cultivation involved the practitioners' recognition of egocentric impulses and their removal through the extirpation of the habits—physical and mental—nurturing them. References to such introspection appear throughout the text of the constitution. Basically the constitution maintained that if the monarch and the courtiers would align themselves with Buddhist virtues, egocentricity would disappear and national harmony could reign. Like Queen Śrīmālā, a devoted Buddhist monarch could set the example and establish the ideal conditions for everyone to follow the Buddhist path to harmony. At least in theory, the constitution made this Buddhist-style introspection and self-control mandatory—integrating it into a larger framework that justified why Japan should be under the aegis of a Buddhist monarch like his aunt.

By the time of *Kojiki* and *Nihonshoki*, therefore, Confucian and

Buddhist state ideologies were already in place. One purpose of *Kojiki* and *Nihonshoki* was to fill out the picture with a distinctively Shinto rationale. According to the Shinto narratives, the *kami* created the world by three means: intentionally by giving structure to primordial ooze; fortuitously by parthenogenesis; and sexually by having off-spring. The politically crucial message of the narrative is that the sun *kami*, Amaterasu, was in charge of the final stages of the creation and administration of Japan. She subsequently delegated her grandson, Ninigi, to perform the latter task, and his great-grandson, Jimmu, would be the legendary first Japanese emperor. Since then, the narratives explain, there has been a continuous family lineage of emperors and empresses up to the present. (In contrast to China, the official Japanese position even today is that the same family has ruled continuously since creation. There has been only one "dynasty" in Japan.) Therefore, according to this Shinto ideology of imperial sovereignty, the Japanese monarchs rule because of their direct, familial relation to the celestial *kami* of creation, especially Amaterasu. This intimate relation with the *kami* trumps the Confucian idea that the sovereign rules by being in accord with heavenly pattern. A divine blood tie (ultimately connected to a *tama* tie) establishes rulership in Japan, and such rulership is not subject to performance evaluation. Hence, by Shinto teachings, no revolt against the throne could ever be justified. Of course, all human beings owe their existence to the *kami*, but the Japanese imperial family is, again, a holographic focal point. Through them the Japanese people, it is assumed, can discover their own inherent links with *kami*. In sharing the *tama* of the imperial ancestors, the emperor or empress shares in the ancestral *tama* of all Japanese—or even of all the world.

Throughout much of their history, the Japanese considered the three justifications for imperial authority—Confucian, Buddhist, and Shinto—to be complementary. Emperors could, for instance, practice Buddhism as well as perform rites as the chief priests for Shinto. To take one example: Emperor Shōmu, the genius behind the international publicity campaign for Japan in the mid-eighth century, even went so far as to be ordained a Buddhist layperson in front of the Great Buddha sculpture he had commissioned for Nara's Great Temple to the East, Tōdai-ji. In so doing, he was affirming through his praxis that Shinto and Buddhism were not at odds. Furthermore, although the Confucian subordination of the emperor to the heavenly mandate never occurred in Japan, every Japanese person below the emperor, including all the courtiers and bureaucrats of the state, was expected to follow Confucian rules of appropriate behavior, including full loyalty to the emperor. Even this loyalty took on a coloration steeped in Shinto narrative, however. Traditional Confucianism in China distinguishes between loyalty of subject to sovereign and loyalty of child to parent. In the Japanese case, though, the intimate connection between the *kami* and the Japanese people collapses the two when it comes to loyalty toward the emperor. The Japanese emperor or empress is both the political sovereign in a hierarchical system and the head of the "Japanese family." Thus, in the Japanese understanding, loyalty to the emperor is itself the highest form of filial piety.

The synergy among the Confucian, Buddhist, and Shinto state ideologies operated on the symbolic level as well. The "heaven" referred to in the Seventeen-Article Constitution uses the same Chinese-derived character as the *"ama"* in the name of the sun *kami*, Amaterasu. Furthermore, when the first article of the constitution stresses the importance of "harmony," the word used is the Japanese *"wa,"* a term also serving in that era as an epithet for Japan. Thus the polysemous nature of the word *"wa"* refers to both the Confucian sense of harmony and the emerging Japanese state. In using such terminology, the constitution is able to blend Confucian and indigenous ideals.

A further example of syncretism is found in the details of Emperor Shōmu's construction of the Great Temple to the East in Nara. Before starting construction, he reportedly sent an emissary to Amaterasu's shrine at Ise to secure the *kami*'s approval. In turn, he decided the "Great Sun Buddha" should be the main Buddha of the temple and ultimately of the state. Furthermore, in taking his own lay Buddhist ordination at this same temple, Shōmu chose an ordination name that was a variant of the Sun Buddha's name. Obviously Shōmu was using the sun symbol from both traditions to lend further authority to his reign.

To sum up: the eighth-century ideology of imperial rule developed in a way that set the throne as a holographic focal point reflecting the whole of Japanese religious philosophy—Confucian, Buddhist, and

Shinto. As Japanese civilization developed, the Confucian system tended to dominate the government institution and its laws including the rules of behavior for the court and the bureaucracy below the level of emperor or empress. Buddhism maintained its emphasis on the inner life and personal cultivation: the ruler should have compassion for the people and ensure fairness to all; the loyal subjects should use Buddhist practices to achieve an egoless commitment to national harmony. For justifying the cosmic and familial aspects of the imperial system, various Shinto elements were emphasized, many of them embedded in the narratives of *Nihonshoki* and *Kojiki*. The two texts lent Shinto its own origin myth and outlined a cosmological system wherein *kami* were deities directly linked to Japan through the imperial family.

In these ancient Shinto developments we find the basis for establishing an essentialist Shinto spirituality as a (if not *the*) state religion. We can easily construct the basis for such an ideological argument to be propagated among the Japanese people. It would go something like this:

> As explained in *Nihonshoki* and *Kojiki*, you are indebted to the *kami* deities for your personal existence and the existence of your world. Given this dependence, you are internally related to the *kami* deities. The emperors and empresses are the direct descendants of these *kami*, and given their special role it is through them you contact your link with the *kami*. Therefore, if you are Japanese, you must be Shinto; if you are Shinto, you owe absolute allegiance to the emperors or empresses and to the government serving them.

Given the standard account of Shinto presented at the opening of this chapter, one might assume that such an argument was forcefully made and that essentialist Shinto spirituality predominated in Japan from this time forward. Such an essentialist Shinto spirituality would claim that people are *born* Shinto because their very existence is the effluent of the celestial creator *kami*. Assuming this metaphysical essence, Shinto would be in the position to prescribe how people should act. The argument would be: to deny imperial rule is to not be Shinto, to not be essentially Japanese, perhaps even to not be human at all. The

Shinto justification of imperial rule could become, in effect, a Japanese equivalent to the Western notion of the divine right of kingship.

This is not what occurred, however. In fact, the kind of argument theoretically posed here was not to gain any prominent influence for a thousand years. Contrary to expectations, a more existential, rather than essentialist, form of Shinto spirituality became the norm. What happened? This is the topic addressed in the next chapter: the second crucial phase in Shinto development.

CHAPTER 4

From Nara to Norinaga (794—1801)

The Pathfinders

In the previous chapter we surveyed the first phase in the evolution of Shinto, identifying various cultural, religious, philosophical, and political dimensions of its development. Much of the indigenous Shinto-related spirituality was obviously consistent with aspects of the contemporary Shinto spirituality analyzed in chapters 1 and 2. It affirmed resonance with, for example, natural forces, spirits, deities, ghosts, and other mysterious phenomena. It placed emphasis on regional *kami,* sacred sites, and rituals of purification. Early Shinto participated fully in a world filled with *kami* and *tama.* As we have seen, however, when Japan became increasingly unified as a country, it also developed a central political organization focused on the imperial family. By the eighth century it was formally using Shinto narratives and symbols to buttress imperial authority, and it would seem that the essentialist Shinto spirituality was on the way to predominating. Conditions changed, however, and it was the existential mode of Shinto spirituality that became more pervasive. Essentialist Shinto spirituality did not disappear, of course, but except for certain localized and sporadic appearances it remained for the most part dormant. The major contravening factor inhibiting its growth was the introduction of esoteric Buddhism and the Buddhist-Shinto syncretism it fostered.

Buddhist-Shinto Syncretism

When Buddhism entered Japan in the sixth century, the country was just beginning to become literate. (At this point, literacy meant using the Chinese written language.) As discussed earlier, Shinto or "proto-Shinto," as we might call the tradition before its contact with Buddhism, was mainly an indigenous, animistic nature religion. It had no written texts and no philosophical tradition. In fact, even its mythic narratives probably varied from region to region and *uji* to *uji*. Buddhism, by contrast, entered Japan with over a thousand years of philosophical development in India, China, and Korea. (Tibetan and Southeast Asian developments were not overtly part of the mix.) Buddhism also brought with it architecture, painting, sculpture, music, and highly elaborate rituals associated with thaumaturgy or wonderworking. Buddhist meditation practices and theory lent the Japanese an enriched insight into their inner selves and psychological motives. With such cultural advantages, one might expect that Buddhism would inevitably displace Shinto as readily as, say, Christianity had overwhelmed the Druids in the British Isles. This is not what happened. Instead Buddhism, in a roundabout way, helped preserve many ancient Shinto values and practices. In so doing, however, it also short-circuited some of the essentialist tendencies emergent in Shinto spirituality. Let us examine this process more closely.

Several schools of Buddhism entered Japan between the sixth and eighth centuries. And, as we have seen, political rulers like Shōtoku and Shōmu utilized them to support their respective regimes. Shōtoku did so by syncretizing Confucian and Buddhist teachings; Shōmu primarily did so by melding Buddhist and Shinto symbols. To understand Buddhist-Shinto syncretism in the ensuing centuries, it is important to notice how Shōtoku's and Shōmu's strategies for synthesis differed. Shōtoku's Seventeen-Article Constitution synthesized Buddhism and Confucianism by establishing an external relation between the two. Each tradition retained its identity and independence by being assigned a different domain of authority. As we have seen, the constitution, on the one hand, prescribed the proper social and political behavior for courtiers and bureaucrats in Confucian terms. On the other hand, it used Buddhist principles and practices to advocate the development of inner awareness and the control of ego. Obviously the two were complementary insofar as an egoless Buddhist would not object to following Confucian proprieties. Yet the complementarity allows the Confucian aspect to remain completely Confucian and the Buddhist aspect completely Buddhist. The integrity of each tradition was not penetrated by the other tradition, and their interface was negotiated by giving each its own sphere of influence. It was as if Shōtoku was working out a contract or treaty between the two imported traditions.

When Emperor Shōmu melded Buddhism with Shinto a century and a half later, however, his synthesis nurtured an internal relation between the two. He had discovered an overlap in the symbol systems of the two traditions: the spirituality of the sun. For Shinto this spirituality lay in the sun *kami*, Amaterasu. This was especially important to Shōmu because *Kojiki* and *Nihonshoki* (written just a few decades earlier) had formally promulgated the familial connection between Amaterasu and the imperial line. For the Buddhist side of the equation, Shōmu knew that the Kegon school, one of the most prominent Buddhist groups in Nara, considered the Sun Buddha to be the basic spiritual principle of the whole cosmos. In Japanese the Sanskrit name (Mahāvairocana or just Vairocana) was either transliterated in various ways or translated as "Dainichi" (Great Sun). As we have seen, when Shōmu built Nara's Great Temple to the East (Tōdai-ji) in the mid-eighth century, he assigned the temple to the Kegon school, cast the monumental bronze image of the Great Sun Buddha, and took for himself a lay ordination name using a variant appellation for the same Buddha. In short: through his very person and practice, he himself embodied the common symbolic ground between Buddhism and Shinto. In effect, he made himself a holographic entry point for the intersection of the two traditions. Through such a tactic he could be the chief priest of Shinto—a direct descendant of the sun *kami*—while simultaneously being an ordained Buddhist layman.

A synthesis through symbolic manipulation and ritual praxis is not the same as a philosophical argument, however. The justification of a praxis—explaining why it works—is a philosophical enterprise known as "metapraxis." Shōmu's synthesis had left the metapractical problem of why the synthesis had efficacy. Shinto narratives about Amaterasu were completely different from Buddhist narratives about Dainichi. So in what precise sense could they be considered the same? There was a need for a philosophical argument to support the claim that Shinto and Buddhism are compatible. When it came to philosophical argument, though, Shinto was at a decided disadvantage vis-à-vis Buddhism and Confucianism, each a tradition with over a millennium of doctrinal and textual development on the mainland. Shinto was an offshoot of the indigenous religions in Japan, and Japan itself had by Shōmu's time only been literate for less than three centuries. And even this literacy had been almost exclusively Chinese, the canonical language for Confucianism and Buddhism in Japan. Writing in Japanese had begun only a few decades earlier with the compiling of *Kojiki,* and the orthography used was, to say the least, cumbersome. So if one were going to develop a metapractical justification for Buddhist-Shinto syncretism, it would not likely come from Shinto. Buddhism, though, did have a vested interest in making the synthesis work and commanded the intellectual resources to do so. This was especially true at the beginning of the ninth century when a new form of Buddhism came into Japan in full force: esotericism.

Esoteric Buddhism's Role in Syncretism

Esotericism was central to both Buddhist traditions ascendant in the Heian period (794–1185): Shingon and Tendai. Shingon is an exclusively esoteric school founded in Japan by Kūkai (774–835) whereas Tendai, founded in Japan by Saichō (766–822), includes esotericism as part of its grand synthesis of many Buddhist perspectives. Although several Buddhist schools had entered Japan by the end of the Nara period, for the most part none had developed into fully independent, religious establishments in their own right. That is: Shingon and Tendai were the first to flourish and develop as distinctively Japanese independent schools. Furthermore, both schools developed forms of Buddhist-Shinto synthesis. Both Shingon and Tendai arose about the time the capital moved from Nara to Kyoto (called "Heian" at the time). Their success was due in part to the fact that Buddhist esotericism shares central assumptions with early Japanese spirituality. With its centuries of doctrinal and practical development on the mainland, esoteric Buddhism was uniquely positioned to give early Shinto spirituality a full-blown philosophical justification, albeit admittedly a justification in Buddhist garb. Let us consider three points where the worldviews of ancient Shinto and esoteric Buddhism intersected— areas of similarity on which Shingon and Tendai Buddhism were able to capitalize.

First, for both early Shinto and Buddhist esotericism, the world is alive with spirituality, as there is no sharp divide between spirit and matter. On the one hand, Shinto affirms the *kami*-filled or *tama*-energized nature of the world. On the other, esoteric Buddhists understand the cosmos as the self-expressive activity of the Cosmic Buddha (Sanskrit: *dharmakāya;* Japanese: *hosshin*). The Cosmic Buddha is not the creator of the cosmos but the cosmos itself. In Buddhism, the "person" is defined in terms of interdependent activities and processes; there is no independent essence or soul behind it. If the cosmos is an interlinked set of processes, therefore, it is a small leap to think of it as "personal" in the Buddhist sense of the word: the world is the Cosmic Buddha's "thought, word, and deed." Like the Kegon Buddhists, Shingon's personal name for this Cosmic Buddha is "Dainichi," the "Great Sun" Buddha—that is, the Great Buddha whose image sits in Nara's Great Temple to the East. As we have explained, Emperor Shōmu had already formally associated the Sun Buddha with Amaterasu, the Shinto sun *kami.* So on this point the two traditions already shared common ground.

Second, Buddhism and early Shinto both stressed the purely mindful heart. In Shinto, this is the *makoto no kokoro* discussed in chapter 1. Mahayana Buddhism, of which esoteric Buddhism can generally be considered a branch, emphasizes the person's ability to achieve or realize the "Buddha's (or awakened) mindful heart." In practical terms this means enlightenment is available to anyone who eliminates ego-centered desires and habits. In esoteric Buddhism, the praxis for achieving this state involves sacramental rituals. Even though the Shingon praxis differed from Shinto's, there was similarity in their emphasis on repetitive mind/body performance such as chanting and gestures. Therefore the Buddhist theories justifying their own ritualistic practices—Shingon metapraxis—could be adjusted to embrace many Shinto practices as well. For example, both early Shinto and esoteric Buddhism assume that certain voiced sounds or words contain transformative power. Esoteric Buddhism refers to this as the "mysterious intimacy of speech" *(gomitsu);* Shinto calls it the "spirit of words" *(kotodama).* This assumption informs both esoteric Buddhist mantra practice and Shinto *norito* practice. In his Shingon Buddhist theory, Kūkai justified the use of mantras in his metaphysical discussion of cosmic and microcosmic "resonance." According to Kūkai, the cosmos (that is, the Buddha Dainichi) chants the mantra and the practitioner's chanting harmonizes with it, thus achieving the "mysterious intimacy of speech." A Shinto thinker could readily adapt the Shingon account to give a metapractical explanation of how sacred words function in Shinto prayer *(norito)* as well. The similarity in assumptions and praxis between Buddhist mantra and Shinto *norito* underscores the importance of the practitioner's enlightened or pure mindful heart. In both cases, the practitioner permeates and is permeated by a holistic sacred mystery. The ideal practitioner is a part containing the whole. The voiced praxis becomes a holographic entry point reflecting the resonance of the universe. In short: in philosophically justifying its own practice (in developing Buddhist metapraxis), esoteric Buddhism brought to Japan a philosophical understanding that could work equally well for Shinto praxis related to *kotodama* and *norito.*

There is, as well, a third commonality: both esoteric Buddhism and early Shinto assume the sacred can be in the form of celestial deities (in Shinto, the *kami* deities; in esoteric Buddhism, the celestial buddhas and bodhisattvas). This allowed correlations between the celestial personages of the two traditions. We have already discussed Emperor Shōmu's linking himself to both the Sun Buddha and the sun *kami.* This correlation process was eventually extended to all the major *kami* and celestial buddhas/bodhisattvas. Moreover, neither esoteric Buddhism nor early Shinto believed the sacred mystery is limited to celestial deities. Any particular thing in the world—a natural object, for example—can also be an entry point into the sacred holograph. We have noted already the Shinto identification of natural objects as *kami.* Shingon's Japanese founder, Kūkai, developed the central principle that "every phenomenon—as the activity of the Cosmic Buddha— preaches the truth" *(hosshin seppō).* In Tendai Buddhism, there was also an exoteric variant of the same notion, namely, that "buddhanature" is in all beings, even insentient ones. Based on such overlaps, Buddhism and Shinto (that is, "Shinto" as the post-Buddhist development of "proto-Shinto") could peacefully coexist in an internal relationship with each other.

To understand how the Buddhist-Shinto synthesis went beyond Emperor Shōmu's simple exchange of sun symbols, let us examine the specific metapractical theory that explained the melding of the celestial buddhas and *kami* deities. Building on ideas implicit in the early Japanese esoteric Buddhist thinkers like Kūkai of the Shingon sect and Saichō of the Tendai sect, esoteric Buddhism formulated in the tenth century an argument for identifying the celestial *kami* with celestial buddhas and bodhisattvas. The theory was called *"honji suijaku."* The *honji suijaku* theory was an extension of the idea that the universe is really the activity of the Cosmic Buddha and that everything we think of as the cosmos is only the symbolic expression of this activity. Hence all the various buddhas and bodhisattvas are ultimately symbolic expressions, almost like emanations, of the single Cosmic Buddha. For esoteric Buddhism, the "ground of reality" *(honji)* is Buddha-filled; but this ground has "traces" *(suijaku)* giving us the *kami*-filled world of Shinto belief. By this reasoning, the various *kami* are surface manifestations of buddhas existing on a deeper level of reality (which are themselves emanating from the Cosmic Buddha). The *honji suijaku* theory was, therefore, an explanation of how a universal (Buddhist) reality could become localized as a Japanese (Shinto) reality. This is fully in accord with the more traditional esoteric Buddhist belief that the entire cosmos is the Cosmic Buddha and the world as we know it is the manifestation of the activities of this buddha. Esoteric Buddhists use mandalas to portray how all buddhas emanate from the Cosmic Buddha (usually considered Dainichi). In accord with the *honji suijaku* theory, so-called *suijaku* art developed similar mandalas with *kami* portrayed in place of the buddhas. This usually meant that Amaterasu replaced Dainichi at the mandala's center, suggesting in effect that all the *kami* emanated from her. In short: esoteric Buddhist theory tended to fuse with traditional Shinto beliefs by intellectually assimilating it, making it a manifestation—but only one manifestation—within the broader Buddhist worldview.

In medieval Japan there were Shinto rebuttals to this Buddhist absorption of Shinto. But for the most part they were ineffectual because they usually did no more than reverse the priority. That is: they argued the *kami* were foundational and the buddhas mere manifestations of them. There were two problems with this approach. First, since by then the Buddhist assimilation was already well entrenched, it could gather little momentum beyond the halls of the major Shinto centers like Ise (home of the Watarai Shinto thinkers who typically made this kind of claim). Second, while the emanation model behind the *honji suijaku* theory is consistent with a long tradition in Buddhism concerning the Cosmic Buddha, there is no comparable emanation theory in ancient Shinto. There is nothing like it in *Nihonshoki* or *Kojiki*, for example, at least not obviously. (There is a sense in which there may be a parallel, however, a point that will have relevance in our discussions of Hirata Shinto in chapter 5.) Thus in the final analysis, such Shinto arguments paradoxically resorted to Buddhist theories in justifying the claim that Shinto is more fundamental than Buddhism. Specifically: only because Amaterasu is identified with Dainichi can Shinto justify a mandala with all the *kami* emanating outward from her. There is no indigenous Shinto text or tradition that would justify such a practice: the ancient Japanese texts had explicitly stated there were many celestial *kami* who existed before Amaterasu. One could say that only by becoming a buddha (the Cosmic Buddha Dainichi) could Amaterasu legitimately be considered the ground of all *kami*.

As it was, however, there were advantages in this alliance for both religions. For Buddhism there were, first of all, obvious political benefits. As we have seen, the eighth-century Japanese court had developed a state ideology justifying imperial rule with a tripod having Confucian, Shinto, and Buddhist legs. To flourish as new Buddhist sects, Shingon and Tendai needed the Heian court to underwrite the infrastructure for intensive doctrinal training and elaborate ritualistic praxis. For the esoteric Buddhists to distance themselves from Shinto, or even worse to brazenly oppose Shinto, would cut off the new sects from one of the three supports for the newly institutionalized state ideology—not a prudent strategy. Moreover, the complex doctrines of Shingon and Tendai were accessible to hardly anyone but the educated elite. By intimately connecting its spirituality with Shinto, however, esoteric Buddhism seemed a praxis less alien to the everyday concerns of commoners. That is: in terms of spiritual dynamics, the world of Shinto's awe-inspiring mystery is almost the same as the world of Buddhism's esotericism. In both cases, the point of praxis is to reconnect with spiritual power (*tama* or, in the case of Shingon, the *"kaji"* of Dainichi Buddha). Buddhism could, therefore, regard an illiterate peasant's practice of visiting a *kami* shrine as spiritually Buddhist but lacking Buddhism's sophisticated metaphysical and metapractical interpretations of how and why that practice works. In the final analysis this approach allowed Buddhism not to oppose, but indeed to co-opt, many performances of Shinto spirituality.

The alliance had advantages for Shinto as well. Through its synergy with esoteric Buddhism, the ancient Shinto worldview could immediately gain the benefit of sophisticated Buddhist analysis, terminology, and argument. Esoteric Buddhism's metaphysics, its metapractical justification of ritual, and its emphasis on the metaphysical fluidity of symbolic forms could be adjusted to support Shinto as well. This was helpful in allowing Shinto spirituality to withstand the onslaught of mainland Confucian and (to a much lesser extent) Daoist intellectualism. From our vantage point twelve centuries later and our knowledge of the important role Shinto would play in subsequent Japanese history, it is easy to overlook Shinto's vulnerability at the beginning of the ninth century. So let us review Shinto's status at that point. First, only two centuries earlier Shōtoku had endorsed a constitution based on Confucian and Buddhist principles, making virtually no direct mention of Shinto at all. Second, the textual form of the Shinto creation narrative and its endorsement of the imperial system were but a century old. There was at this point still no viable system for writing in Japanese, the language of the indigenous oral spiritual tradition. (In fact, legend attributes the invention of the eventually standard writing system to Kūkai, the founder of Shingon Buddhism.) Third, just five decades earlier, after the writing of *Nihonshoki* and *Kojiki*, Emperor Shōmu—the chief priest of Shinto—had taken a Buddhist initiation. And fourth, over the previous two centuries the government had increasingly put into place Chinese, Confucian-related, bureaucratic structures for running the state. Following the Chinese model, to secure a position in this bureaucracy one had to show mastery in Confucian classics as taught in the official "college" of the empire. In the face of such challenges, Shinto could have easily disappeared, at least for the elite, educated segments of the society. By engaging in the syncretism with Buddhism, however, Shinto practitioners could go on practicing as they had always done—but now with the endorsement of Buddhist philosophy to make it respectable in the eyes of intellectuals steeped in Chinese thought.

Ryōbu Shinto as a Syncretistic Paradigm

Let us consider one example of how this merger with esoteric Buddhism was institutionalized. Both Shingon and Tendai Buddhism developed their own form of syncretism with Shinto. For simplicity's sake, let us just focus here on the Shingon version, Ryōbu Shinto. It adapted the dual *(ryōbu)* mandala system of Shingon Buddhism to represent relations among *kami* deities. The mandalas are graphic depictions using the whole-in-every-part paradigm, and mandalic practices serve as holographic entry points into the sacred. The mandala-based theory portrayed a basic cosmic power manifesting itself as the myriad individual buddhas. Ryōbu Shinto followed this paradigm in explaining how the universal *kami* and *tama* (so important to everyday Shinto praxis) can be related to the personal celestial *kami* deities (so crucial to the Shinto ideology supporting imperial rule). This interpretation resulted in mandalas of the form mentioned earlier wherein Amaterasu sits at the center surrounded by the other *kami.*

Hence Ryōbu Shinto became a form of Shinto praxis that could be performed in Shingon temple precincts without much concern about whether the practice was "Shinto" or "Buddhist." Exemplifying how far this syncretism extended, even the Outer and Inner Shrines of Ise —one of the most sacred sites of Shinto—were interpreted in terms of the dual mandalas of Shingon Buddhism: the Diamond and the Womb. Hence, through syncretistic forms like Ryōbu Shinto, Buddhism and Shinto could be, if not completely integrated, at least interlinked enough to share geographical, ritual, and spiritual space. This syncretism is visible even in the case of the Osorezan shamans discussed in chapter 3. Traditionally the blind shamans spent decades in esoteric practices at a Tendai Buddhist temple. Yet their initiation involved "marrying" a mountain *kami,* and their practices included the chanting of ancient Shinto *norito.*

Before going further, let us summarize the impact of esoteric Buddhism on Shinto. At the opening of this chapter, there was the suggestion that Shinto was not superseded by the introduction of a highly developed mainland religion as, for example, Druidism had been supplanted by Christianity in the British Isles. Buddhism's strategy was instead to assimilate and subordinate Shinto without obliterating it. Consequently Shinto did not have to justify itself against Buddhism. The esoteric Buddhist and Shinto worldviews were sufficiently compatible that Shinto could rely on Buddhist arguments for its own conceptual articulations if needed. As we have seen, for example, a Shinto thinker would not have to develop an argument for the reality of *kotodama* if esoteric Buddhist philosophy had already "proved" the interdependent resonance between reality and the voicing of words. If some philosopher doubted basic Shinto views on reality, a defense could be mounted by shifting the Buddhist justification of mantra practice to one justifying the sacred incantations of *norito*. This meant that Shinto did not have to develop ex nihilo a philosophical system of its own.

In fact, in this new syncretistic context in which Shinto and Buddhism were so intimately related there was barely a need for the separate term "Shinto" at all. As mentioned earlier, the word "Shinto," or at least the concept of a discrete Shinto spiritual tradition, arose in ancient Japan as a way of distinguishing the *kami*-based religion from the imported religion of Buddhism. Not surprisingly, then, with syncretism as the norm, the term "Shinto" had no popular use in Japan until the development of state ideology in the middle of the nineteenth century. In that era, an essentialist Shinto spirituality was on the rise and the agenda was to separate "real" Shinto from its Buddhist "distortions." Because of Buddhist-Shinto syncretism, however, it seems that for a thousand years of Japanese history most people did not ordinarily find it useful to distinguish "Shinto" from "Buddhist." These people did all along refer to "*kami*," of course, but they knew that on some level (perhaps understood only by intellectuals) *kami* were just alternative forms of buddhas.

Buddhist-Shinto syncretism became the predominant religion in Japan. With core Shinto ideas and values assuming an esoteric Buddhist coloration, it became difficult for Shinto to maintain much of an independent presence and it seemed in many cases to be overshadowed by the Buddhist side of the syncretism. Confucianism in this period suffered a different fate. Empowered with spirituality from two traditions, the Buddhist-Shinto amalgam practically displaced any remnants of Japanese Confucianism as a vital *spiritual* tradition. Confucianism remained important, but mainly as the font of moral and social virtue learned through the study of Chinese classics. Knowledge of these classics was still required of the male courtiers and literati. Although the Confucian terminology for social relations had become an integral part of the courtly vocabulary, there was little effort at innovation to make Confucianism more suitable to Japan (as Buddhism had done). In general, there would be little creative Confucian thought again in Japan until the sixteenth century. Until then, Buddhism ruled the spiritual and intellectual landscapes of Japan.

The Rise and Fall of Buddhist Hegemony

Vitalized with its syncretistic absorption of Shinto, Buddhism was the principal form of philosophical discourse in Japan from about 800 to 1600. But Buddhism was not monolithic throughout this period. Tendai and Shingon, for example, did not retain their dominance. In the twelfth and thirteenth centuries, the Kamakura-period religions of Pure Land, Zen, and Nichiren blossomed in Japan. Although these new forms of Japanese Buddhism were not technically esoteric traditions, they did share the basic vision of spirituality as inherent in all things. They preserved the assumption that all things are expressive of the Cosmic Buddha or that all things share in a root enlightenment of some sort. Therefore, for the most part, these new religions shared the three points of commonality with Shinto we discussed in relation to esoteric Buddhism: the omnipresence of spirit in matter; the importance of the pure mindful heart; and the intermediating role of celestial beings. If anything, their major difference from Shingon and Tendai was in simplifying praxis away from the elaborate rituals of esotericism. But as we have seen, simplicity is a Shinto virtue as well.

Consequently, up to the end of the sixteenth century Shinto had Buddhism for its intellectual guardian against philosophical attacks. This is not to say there was no doctrinal development in Shinto during the medieval period. As some shrines gained in popularity and prestige, often as sites of major pilgrimage or festivals, they created their own study centers for training priests. Many larger shrines also developed their own philosophical understandings and promulgated them through branch shrines in other regions of the country. Two of the most influential sects of Shinto were Watarai (associated with the

Outer Shrine at Ise) and Yoshida (associated with the Yoshida and Hirano shrines). In fact, there were at times points of contention between Shinto and Buddhism in the period before 1600. We have already noted that Watarai Shinto critiqued and tried to reverse the Buddhist *honji suijaku* theory—the basic principle used to justify Buddhism's absorption of Shinto. It was later joined in this critique by the Yoshida sect, which also explicitly criticized the Buddhist foundations of Ryōbu Shinto. If we were to look for traces of essentialist Shinto spirituality during the medieval period, these would be two likely sites.

Generally, however, the debates between the Buddhist and Shinto establishments in this era were between two views that were close rather than diametrically opposed. For the most part, the medieval Shinto philosophical critiques of Buddhist teachings did not have much influence beyond the priesthood of major shrines and their branches. That is: there was no significant nationwide Shinto philosophical system. As a result, most Shinto practice continued to flourish within Buddhist precincts while the large Shinto shrines without Buddhist affiliation went their separate ways. This relation continued until the Tokugawa and modern periods. Only then do we find the major divorce of Shinto from Buddhism as part of a renewed essentialist Shinto movement. Let us now consider how this movement began.

We start with the cultural dynamics of Tokugawa or Edo Japan (1603–1868). For our account, two circumstances were crucial—one political and one intellectual. The political circumstance was that after centuries of internal warfare a new shogun, Tokugawa Ieyasu (1543–1616), had unified Japan in such a way that his family would continue their political control of the country for more than 250 years. Although the sixteenth century had been a major era for exchange with the West, once the Tokugawa shoguns secured their power they virtually closed Japan to the outside world. Consequently, until the entrance of Commodore Perry's gunboats into Tokyo Bay in 1853, the major dynamics of political change during the Tokugawa era were internal to the country. The Tokugawa ruled so successfully because they were adept at strategies of institutional governance that would keep at bay their various potential enemies: feudal barons, samurai, peasants, merchants, and religious leaders.

This is a good place to discuss the general erosion in the power of the Japanese emperor that had begun as early as the ninth century. Throughout the Heian period (794–1185), the emperors remained the titular heads of state but in fact were often quite effete. Powerful aristocratic families (mainly the Fujiwara) actually ruled from behind the throne, often maintaining control by intermarriage into the imperial family. Indeed, in the tenth and eleventh centuries the Fujiwara typically managed to force emperors to abdicate the throne when they reached the age of maturity. This policy ensured that a Fujiwara uncle of a child emperor would hold the office of regent and be the de facto ruler of Japan. As the nobles focused on living the refined, aesthetic life of the court in Kyoto, they increasingly turned over the administration of baronies throughout Japan to samurai administrators.

By the end of the twelfth century, these samurai had turned against their noble patrons and then vied with each other for control of Japan. The winners of these wars became the generalissimo (usually called "shogun"), the leader of the administrative government (often called the *"bakufu"*) for all Japan. Again, the emperor was always given deference as titular head of state but had (with some short-lived exceptions) almost no genuine political initiative. A military aristocracy had replaced the noble aristocracy as the real power in Japan, and the military leaders were even less disposed than the nobles to pretend the emperor was really in charge. Thus the *bakufu* did not even feel the need to operate out of the capital, Kyoto. Instead they stayed close to their home domains where they could count on stable alliances with neighboring warlords. In the twelfth century, for example, Kamakura became the center of government administration while the emperor remained in Kyoto, the official capital.

After another particularly chaotic and bloody period with no generalissimo in charge (called the Sengoku or "Warring Provinces" period: 1467–1568), Oda Nobunaga (1534–1582) established control of much of central Japan. He was followed by Toyotomi Hideyoshi (1537–1598) and then the previously mentioned Ieyasu. By the time of Ieyasu, the entire country was unified under his hegemony and he took the title of "shogun." He established his governmental headquarters in Edo (present-day Tokyo) and built a social system of such stability that his Tokugawa descendants ruled Japan up to 1868. As had been the case for many centuries, the emperor continued to reign without ruling and the Tokugawa shoguns continued to grant the throne their formal deference. As under all the other shoguns, Tokugawa rule was based shamelessly on the authority of the sword—not the intellectual foundation of Shinto, Buddhism, and Confucianism that had buttressed imperial rule in the early centuries of Japan. In this respect the emperors retained some religious charisma, but the shogunate successfully denied this charisma any significant political leverage.

Religion was a particularly thorny issue that Ieyasu's two military predecessors, Nobunaga and Hideyoshi, had already begun to address. Collectively the policies of the three successive generalissimos led to the following situation. First, the upstart religion from the West, Christianity, was banned. The small numbers of Christians who refused to renounce their faith had to go underground. The squelching of the Christian movement in Japan was the precursor of closing Japan off from almost all contact with the outside world. This policy was initiated in 1639 and officially continued through 1854. Second, the Tendai Buddhist main temple on Kyoto's Mount Hiei had grown to be the most powerful religious institution in Japan. In 1571 Nobunaga burned down the complex, destroying its three thousand buildings and its army of ten thousand warrior monks. Third, the most populist Buddhist religion of the time, the Shin Buddhist Honganji sect, had assembled a huge peasant army of its own that Nobunaga defeated in 1580. The sect then underwent a schism in 1603, breaking into Eastern and Western Honganji, thereby dividing the unity of this Buddhist group. And fourth, under Ieyasu the shogunate began to monitor the philosophical-religious schools of scholars, hoping to maintain at least some control over new developments and ideologies. Accompanying these four political events were intellectual circumstances equally important to the future of Shinto.

The key factors of intellectual change came to a head in the late sixteenth century when something philosophically new took hold in Japan. Throughout Japanese history there had been periods when Japanese groups (mainly religious or diplomatic) made the dangerous journey across the stormy Sea of Japan to the mainland, bringing back home cultural innovations and artifacts. In the fifteenth and sixteenth centuries especially, groups of Japanese Buddhist monks, mainly from the Zen tradition, went to the mainland to study. When they returned, they brought with them not only further materials related to Buddhism but also books from other philosophical traditions popular in China at the time. For our present concerns, the most significant items in their cargo were works of Chinese Neo-Confucianism. Although Zen Buddhist monastic scholars were studying the texts and introducing them to Japan, the books contained a philosophical system that would ultimately undermine the intellectual hegemony of Buddhism in the country. Neo-Confucianism was a sophisticated syncretistic philosophical movement in China that enriched traditional Confucian teachings with ideas from Buddhism and Daoism. By incorporating key ideas from these traditions into its own, Neo-Confucianism had disarmed the most powerful Buddhist and Daoist criticisms against Confucianism. As a result, from about the twelfth century up to the early twentieth century, Neo-Confucian philosophy (in various forms) generally dominated the Chinese intellectual scene.

These Neo-Confucian arguments against Buddhism entered Japan just before Tokugawa stability and peace brought rapid urbanization. The growth of city life supported schools of learning outside the traditional Buddhist temple complexes that had trained monk-scholars. The samurai (who needed job retraining to find a useful place in the peacetime society of the Tokugawa bureaucracy) and the aspiring merchant class (who needed to acquire culture fast) frequented such urban schools. Furthermore, the increasingly literate urbanites created a demand for widely distributed, printed publications. By the late seventeenth century, literary culture, including philosophy, was thriving in the cities.

As mentioned earlier, the Tokugawa kept an eye on intellectual developments within their domain. If urbanization and advanced printing techniques made it possible for published works to reach a mass audience, government surveillance and censorship also became easier. Formally the Tokugawa shogunate tended eventually to favor the Neo-Confucian writings of the Japanese Shushi school, based on the ideas of the highly influential Chinese Neo-Confucian philosopher Zhu Xi (1130–1200). The shogunate supported the school by occasionally issuing edicts that its teachings alone defined the ideology of the state. Although other forms of philosophy were supposedly banned, the ban was not enforced energetically. It was probably more a warning shot to alert thinkers from rival schools that Big Brother Tokugawa was watching them.

Why would the shoguns look favorably on Neo-Confucianism? First, as a Confucian tradition it directly supported the ideas of performing one's role within a socially and politically hierarchical society. (In theory but not always practice, Buddhist doctrine favored a democratic spiritual ideal: without distinction in rank or education, everyone shared alike in the primordial ground of enlightenment.) As Japanese society became more urban, it was important for the Tokugawa shogunate to have a value system in place to ensure loyalty to those above: for everyone to know their place. As we have seen, Confucian values had generally performed this role in Japan from as far back as the seventh century and they could do so again. Furthermore, the more successful the Tokugawa peace, the less need there was for the samurai class to be warriors. Acculturating these samurai into the bureaucracy would remove another potential threat to social stability. The Confucian virtues of civil responsibility and loyalty could displace the soldier's virtues of courage and allegiance to one's warlord.

Second, the Tokugawa were uneasy about the potential influence of Buddhism among the people, the clergy, and the educated. As we have seen, Nobunaga and Ieyasu had already dealt with the military power of the major Buddhist institutions. The next step was to put into place institutional strategies for keeping the Buddhists in check more generally. The shogunate was quite creative in its methods. For example, it made Buddhist temples the official census keepers of the nation by requiring every family to enroll in a temple. This was a financial benefit for Buddhist priests who could collect fees for their services and at the same time use their registries as a way of securing clients for their funerary services. All this served to secularize, bureaucratize, and dilute any spiritual fervor within the Buddhist membership—exactly what the shogunate wanted.

And third, intellectually, Buddhism presented a different problem for the Tokugawa. The overwhelming majority of key Japanese thinkers from the early ninth through sixteenth centuries had been affiliated with Buddhism, not Confucianism or Shinto. The major Buddhist temples had supplemented or even eclipsed the imperial court and the shoguns' *bakufu* as centers of intellectual activity. Because the Buddhist centers were scattered all over the country, many in isolated areas far from the cities, they were difficult to monitor from centralized bureaucratic offices. Not requiring remote centers for religious praxis and not needing to function as ritual sites for villagers' religious needs, Neo-Confucian academies could function quite well in the more secular and public environment of the cities, where there was a pool of wealthy potentional clients. Although such urban academies could be politically cantankerous for the shogunate, at least they were close by and could be monitored. The urban academies, therefore, became the new secular centers of philosophical activity.

In summation: by supporting Neo-Confucianism's prepackaged arguments against the Buddhists, by relegating Buddhist temples to bureaucratic census takers, by defanging the Buddhist temples of their military power, and by encouraging the rise of secular urban academies, the Tokugawa were able to undermine Buddhism both institutionally and intellectually. In undermining the philosophical hegemony of Buddhism, however, there was an indirect threat to Shinto. Because of the Buddhist-Shinto syncretism discussed earlier, to attack Buddhist metaphysics and metapraxis was, if indirectly, to attack some fundamentals of Shinto thought as well, at least as formulated since the ninth and tenth centuries. To undermine the Buddhist doctrines of sacred emanation, the spiritual power of voiced words, and the interpenetration of nature, humanity, and spirit, for example, would be to undercut the parallel Shinto theories developed during the heyday of Buddhist-Shinto syncretism. Consequently, with its intellectual critiques of Buddhism, Neo-Confucianism presented Shinto as well with a problem: Neo-Confucianism, this philosophical newcomer in the neighborhood, could apparently intimidate Shinto's intellectual protector, esoteric Buddhism. Unable to depend on Buddhism to back it up intellectually, what could Shinto do?

There were two obvious strategies available. The first is that Shinto could find a new ally—this time syncretizing with (Neo-)Confucianism instead of Buddhism. The second alternative would be to develop a distinctively Shinto philosophy from the ground up, making Shinto a tradition that could hold its own against any other philosophy in

Japan. To some extent, Shinto tried both alternatives. We begin with
the option of Confucian-Shinto syncretism. The second option, building a new philosophical foundation, is addressed in the following
section.

The first Neo-Confucian scholar who tried to become an adviser in
the Tokugawa shogunate was Hayashi Razan (1583–1657). He took
pains to write about Shinto in a favorable way. In his reading of Zhu
Xi, Razan incorporated Shinto's understanding of imperial rule as
well as its emphasis on *kami* in connection with the mindful heart.
Yamazaki Ansai (1619–1682) went so far as to found a new tradition
called Suika (divine grace and protection) Shinto that explicitly advocated the joint study of Neo-Confucianism and Shinto as the path to
virtue. In this context of Confucian-Shinto syncretism, we also might
mention the rise of *bushidō*, "the way of the warrior." When Shinto
values such as genuineness, purity of heart, and imperial rule blended
with Confucian notions of hierarchy (as embedded especially in the
Japanese interpretation of its virtues of filial piety and loyalty), there
was an important side effect outside Neo-Confucian and Shinto institutions per se. A distinctively Japanese understanding of loyalty to
one's lord (and ultimately to the emperor) developed.

This Japanese variant took Confucianism's emphasis on loyalty and
appropriate behavior toward one's superiors and enhanced it with two
Shinto qualities: affect (emotion) and the holographic paradigm. The
affective dimension maintained that loyalty does not derive merely
from formulas about hierarchical roles. This would make loyalty no
more than an external relation. For *bushidō*, loyalty is not role-playing
or fulfilling some social contract. In the new Japanese interpretation,
loyalty derives at least as much from love, an internal relation with the
lord and his house. Such an internal relation reinforces the holographic model of the whole-in-every-part. That is: true loyalty arises
from the sincere mindful heart that recognizes how the house headed
by one's lord is reflected within each of its members, including oneself.
To turn against one's lord is to turn against oneself. In this context,
when a vassal could not agree with and follow the command of his
lord, seppuku—ritualized suicide—was often the only option. By the
holographic model, because the whole is part of the individual, the
individual cannot be fully true to oneself and simultaneously oppose

the whole. The act of seppuku arises from the double bind of being torn between one's own position against the whole and one's identity as reflecting the whole.

Such values found a home in the *bushidō* ideology of Tokugawa Japan. In fact, one founder of the tradition, Yamaga Sokō (1622–1685), studied under Razan and, although he later rejected the Zhu Xi brand of Neo-Confucianism, remained a Confucian of his own sort. He was also a strong nationalist and advocated the uniqueness and sacred quality of the emperor—thereby blending Shinto and Confucian elements. Such use of Shinto elements to develop samurai values would make it easier for the militarists to tap Shinto ideals during the foreign war years from 1894 to 1945.

This historical and intellectual backdrop sheds light, incidentally, on the kamikaze mentality of Japanese pilots in the Pacific War. A common Western interpretation is that the pilots were performing acts of *self-sacrifice* for the emperor. Technically this is not true. The pilots were not denying themselves in order to serve a higher cause. On the contrary, following the holographic reasoning, the whole (the Japanese nation with the emperor as its holographic entry point) is within each loyal Japanese pilot. Their voluntary death affirmed this holographic relation. In effect, by dying for the emperor the kamikaze pilots were dying for themselves. Their act was one of self-affirmation, even self-preservation, not self-denial. In light of this example, we can see how Shinto-Confucian syncretism lay behind the *bushidō* ideals valorized in twentieth-century Japan. (Incidentally, Buddhism's emphasis on self-control and inner discipline also influenced the development of *bushidō* praxis. Although this topic takes us outside our present concerns, it is significant that *bushidō* derived its strength by standing on the ancient tripod of Confucianism, Shinto, and Buddhism.)

Thus far we have seen two philosophical conditions that would set the stage for the radically new state ideology to develop in the nineteenth century. First there was the revitalization of Confucian social values and behavior. This revitalization was selective and, as we saw in the case of loyalty, blended with Japanese cultural interpretations. Second, the *bushidō* value system gave the samurai a new sense of place in peacetime society. They could bring their values from the battlefield to the bureaucratic offices, where dedication, absolute loyalty, and discipline were equally important. *Bushidō* ideology articulated its values into a formal system promulgated beyond the military class itself. That is: the *bushidō* mentality became potentially a model for all Japanese —its elements promulgated in the Japanese public schools of the late nineteenth and early twentieth centuries under the rubric of "moral education." To understand the profound relation between Shinto and state ideology in the nineteenth and twentieth centuries, however, we need to consider one more philosophical condition arising from the late eighteenth century: the new interpretation of Shinto emerging from the Native Studies movement.

Norinaga and the Rise of Native Studies

With the erosion of Buddhist hegemony in Japan's intellectual world, we noted that Shinto logically had two options. One was to ally itself with the new intellectual tradition vying for intellectual dominance— Neo-Confucianism (and the subsequent revival of classic Confucianism as well). The second alternative, we recall, was that Shinto could start from scratch and develop its own philosophical position independent of both Buddhism and Confucianism (and *bushidō,* too, for that matter). This alternative had the more profound influence on Shinto's development in the long run. This was the path followed by the *kokugaku* or "Native Studies" movement. For the development of Shinto doctrine, without question the key figure of the eighteenth century was the Shinto philosopher we have been mentioning intermittently since chapter 1: Motoori Norinaga (1730–1801). He tried to take the Japanese back to the "way of the ancients," the Japanese world before the influence of mainland traditions like Confucianism, Daoism, and Buddhism.

Native Studies did not originate with Norinaga. It had begun a few decades earlier as a strictly literary and philological movement. The purpose of Native Studies was to bring to the study of ancient Japanese texts the methodological sophistication and insight already shown by the Japanese Confucian scholars in studying ancient Chinese classics (so-called *kogaku,* "ancient [Chinese] studies"). Unlike some earlier members of the Native Studies movement, however, Norinaga was a fervent follower of Shinto. In fact, he believed he had been conceived only in response to his parents' prayer at a Shinto shrine. For Norinaga, then, even his very birth showed an intimate connection with awe-inspiring mysterious power. Because of his profound commitment to Shinto, Norinaga turned his philological skills primarily to analyzing, not ancient Japanese poetry (as his predecessors in Native Studies had mainly done), but *Kojiki*.

As discussed in chapter 3, *Kojiki* had been written in an orthographic system so idiosyncratic that parts of it, especially the most ancient Japanese prayers and poems, were almost undecipherable. For centuries it existed as a marginalized text outshone by the Chinese-language *Nihonshoki*. A brilliant philologist impelled by religious intensity, Norinaga became probably the first person in almost a thousand years to be able to decode virtually every word of the book. It took him over three decades to render *Kojiki* into a meticulously annotated text readable to his educated contemporaries. But however arduous the task, Norinaga found his project to be not only philologically but also spiritually rewarding.

When it came to *Kojiki*, Norinaga was a textual literalist—in fact, a fundamentalist of sorts. For him, *Kojiki* was a pure text in at least four respects. First, it was linguistically pure: it preserved the prehistoric forms of the Japanese language. (Remember that the text was supposedly a direct transcription of the most ancient Japanese oral narratives.) Indeed, one of Norinaga's crucial philological insights was that the ancient, preliterate Japanese language included some consonant-vowel combinations not reflected in the ninth-century writing system that eventually became standard. This means that words which eventually became homonyms were not always so. In fathoming the etymological roots of ancient terms, this fact was crucial. Second, he believed *Kojiki* to be textually pure. According to Norinaga, when scribes recopy texts over the generations, they often add or subtract a little something, especially in those places where the text does not seem to make sense as written. For Norinaga, a virtue of the *Kojiki* text was precisely that it was so unreadable. If the copyists could not read the text, there would be no chance of their intentionally rewriting parts to give it more sense. As we will see, this was particularly important to Norinaga because he believed *Kojiki* to be full of awe-inspiring events inexplicable to human reason. Such awe, of course, is the very heart of

Shinto spirituality. Third, the text was culturally pure. Because *Kojiki* purportedly consisted of the most ancient Japanese oral narratives, because it transcribed the oral texts literally, and because there was no attempt, as in the case of the compilers of *Nihonshoki,* to make the text suitable for foreign consumption, it was purely Japanese.

And fourth, the text was religiously pure. *Kojiki* relates the narrative of creation. Since language must go back to the *kami* deities, the original story must have been in the words of the celestial *kami* themselves. According to Norinaga, then, every creation narrative not written in ancient Japanese must already be a translation, if not a transformation, of the true story. Knowing the narrative to be sacred and expressed in the words of the *kami,* the ancient court storytellers handed down the account verbatim from one generation to the next. Emperors, themselves *kami,* appointed these storytellers. Therefore, Norinaga reasoned, the *Kojiki*'s text goes back directly to the words of the *kami* themselves at the creation. To get back to those words—the *kotodama* of their sounds as well as their meaning—would be to participate ritually in the act of the creation itself. In chapter 1 we discussed Norinaga's theory of poetic creativity: the collective resonance of the *kokoro* in events, words, and poet creates the poem. He assumed the creation of the world had the same structure. While the words of the *kami* did not themselves create the world, the words spoken were an intrinsic part of the resonance in that creative moment. For Norinaga, in short, *Kojiki* is a holographic entry point containing in its words the entire *kami*-filled, *tama*-charged world. Its reading (with *makoto no kokoro*) puts one into intimate connection with the ancient ways of the *kami.*

In gathering evidence for the meaning and pronunciation of words in *Kojiki,* Norinaga used *Nihonshoki* as one of his several sources. There was, after all, significant overlap in content between the two works. Yet this joint reading also underscored certain differences between the texts. Where there are deviations between *Nihonshoki* and *Kojiki,* Norinaga's theory could attribute them to a rationalizing "Chinese mentality" instead of a simple acceptance of the original narrative with a sincere mindful heart. For Norinaga, Shinto's goal is to be at home with the sacred mystery all around us. To submit the actions and intentions of the *kami* deities to the criteria of human reason separates us from, rather than intimately connects us with, that awe-inspiring mystery. To interpret the mystery through reason, Norinaga believed, is to objectify the mystery into something external to be studied, killing the resonance of the mindful heart, *kokoro*. To describe mystery so that we can discover our intimate connection with it, it is more important that the description be accurate than reasonable. For Norinaga, the actual words—sounds as well as meanings—are crucial.

One example of a divergence between *Kojiki* and *Nihonshoki* illustrates the kind of difference relevant to this point. Obviously, given the importance of Amaterasu, the sun *kami*, her origins should be unambiguous. Yet the accounts in *Kojiki* and *Nihonshoki* are dissimilar. As we recall from chapter 3, after having sex with Izanagi, Izanami gave birth to the fire *kami* and was severely burned. She passed on to the putrid world of the dead, the Land of Yomi. According to *Kojiki*, Izanagi was so grief stricken at the loss of his wife that he descended to the underworld to bring her back. He found Izanami had been transformed into a decomposing figure accompanied by demons. After fleeing and closing off the gateway to the underworld, Izanagi went to purify himself by bathing in a river (traditionally considered the origin of the water purification rite discussed earlier). In the effluent from washing his left eye, the sun *kami* was born. Obviously this passage describes a wondrous, mysterious sort of birth. *Nihonshoki,* by contrast, claims that Amaterasu was a natural progeny of coitus between Izanagi and Izanami. Indeed it states she was consciously conceived to be the progenitor of the rulers of the earthly realm, the future emperors. The *Nihonshoki* account is rationally more credible and in accord with the human understanding of procreation. Yet Norinaga is skeptical of this kind of reasoning—what he calls the "Chinese mentality." The Chinese mentality attempts to explain away the wondrous by making it conform to human reason.

According to Norinaga, when we use reason to dissolve mystery rather than discover its intimate links with us, we run the risk of distorting the truly wondrous nature of reality. If everything makes sense, there is no room for awe. Norinaga's conviction derives from his own brand of spirituality and trust, but the idea is not so alien to us today as it might first appear. In ordinary parlance, we often accept that "fact is stranger than fiction" or that some account is "strange but true" or even that it is "so incredible, it must be true; nobody could make up a story like that." Robert Ripley made a career of describing "oddities" in his "Believe It or Not" newspaper cartoon strips, television shows, and museums. Ripley's popularity derived from his reputation for accuracy of description—he challenged anyone "to prove him a liar." Yet he seldom if ever explained, let alone explained away, the oddities. Such a common human sensibility that not everything true can be explained lies at the heart of Norinaga's appreciation of Shinto.

Norinaga's methodological and religious assumptions led him to conclusions that were to have a major impact in the ensuing two centuries—and, as a by-product, laid the foundations for a rabid form of ethnocentrism. A literalist with deep spiritual reverence for the *kami*, Norinaga took the *Kojiki* to be a narrative about the creation of not just Japan but the world itself. That is: the *kami* created the whole world. If so, he wondered, why did not all the people on the planet have the genuine creation story? Given his theory that copyists tend to have their copies "make more sense" in each transcribed version, he decided that the creation story must have been further corrupted each time it was written down. Even *Nihonshoki*, which had the *Kojiki* narrative available to it, is not free of such corruption. How much worse would be the distortions occurring in countries more distant from Japan, countries where the Japanese language is unknown? A few small elements might remain, here and there, but many crucial details would be lost. The Japanese, according to Norinaga, had fortuitously written down the original (which is to say *Kojiki*) narrative in a script they themselves would soon not be able to read. Therefore the story remained untouched and pure. For him, *Kojiki* was a time capsule going back to the original creation itself. Through *Kojiki* one could go back to the primal language of creation, the words used in most ancient Japan. All languages, even his contemporary Japanese, are a distortion of those words. Norinaga believed that if people were to go back to those words—their original sounds and meanings—they would experience the spiritual power of words *(kotodama)* and the spirit *(tamashii)* of ancient Japan (Yamato). Through such words people could again interconnect with the awesome mystery of which they are each a part and which, with a pure *kokoro,* they can holistically reflect. Furthermore, Norinaga maintained that in *Kojiki* alone was to be found the true basis for the Japanese imperial system, the only way to social, political, and natural harmony.

For the most part, Norinaga's understanding of Japan's special place in world history was not an agenda of either revolution or world dominance. It was more romantic than that. His spiritual vision pictured a world in which people would live together harmoniously with each other and with nature. He criticized Confucianism, Neo-Confucianism, and Buddhism for their overly rationalized systems of thought. He believed they only led people away from accepting the mystery that allows them to live at home harmoniously in the universe and with each other. Norinaga was equally critical of *bushidō*, the formalized warrior ethos so attractive to samurai and the bureaucrats of the Tokugawa government. The genuine mindful heart, he insisted, is a life-affirming responsiveness and interconnectedness. He would have found the opening line of *Leafy Shadows (Hagakure)*—an early-eighteenth-century canonical text of the *bushidō* tradition—to be completely wrong-headed. Its famous words are: "To be a samurai is to die." In Shinto as he understood it, death is always a defilement, not an ideal. For Norinaga, nothing could be a greater violation of the mindful heart than the valorization of death. The way of the warrior, he reasoned, was a state ideology developed to make people, specifically males, go against their own human nature and the desire to live at home in a world filled with awesome mystery. According to Norinaga, the warrior ideology calls this universally human nature "feminine" *(taoyameburi)* and encourages males to feel superior to it by embracing the warrior ideology, which is "masculine" *(masuraobumi)*. In so doing, *bushidō* leads males to live in ways contrary to their fundamental humanity, eradicating the very possibility of expressing their genuine mindful hearts. Hence there can be no authenticity or sincerity in *bushidō*.

Following this line of reasoning, Norinaga argued that what is most truly human is what the warriors had designated as "feminine." He characterized the authentic human being as someone guided by intuition, not rationalization; by the mindful heart, not the disembodied intellect; by holistic responsiveness, not duty to principles. Such a person is so in touch with others—both people and things—as to be touched by all. Such a person lives in a social community that is at home in the natural world but values social interconnections as much as naturalness. (Norinaga criticized Daoism for undervaluing the social.) For Norinaga, in fact, Japan came close to having such an ideal community in the Heian court, the world that produced such works as *Tale of Genji* and the collections of poems written in native Japanese words. He thought that the aesthetic and the spiritual came together in their appreciation of the "ah-ness of things" *(mono no aware)*. Norinaga's ideal of a "real man" was not the swashbuckling samurai but the Heian court aesthete, sleeves of his kimono unashamedly wet with tears of sensitivity.

Such a romantic vision is a long way from the Japanese ideology of the war years, an ideology supposedly anchored in Shinto values. Norinaga thought he had discovered an ancient path—the way home to traditional Japanese values: sincerity, purity, harmony with nature, the ability to be awestruck, and the precious celebration of life within communities of spiritual and aesthetic sensitivity. In the ensuing century, however, something unforeseen happened. Norinaga had argued for a distinct Shinto essence, distinguishing it from all other religions. By following the trail of Japanese culture back to *Kojiki,* he had returned to the precise point where the seeds of essentialist Shinto spirituality had originally been sown, the seeds that had been dormant for almost a thousand years. His successors then redefined the essence of Shinto to support a militancy that Norinaga could not have imagined let alone advocated. The ancient paths Norinaga had discovered became the blueprint for social engineering. His footpaths of romantic nostalgia would become the guide for ideological bulldozers that would clear the way for modernization, military development, and jingoistic fervor. The ancient path would become a network of limited access highways with heavy tolls. These developments are the topic of our next chapter.

CHAPTER 5

All Roads Lead to Tokyo (1801–2002)
The Highway Engineers

After the death of Motoori Norinaga, the Native Studies movement continued to develop and gain in influence. The Native Studies thinkers were by no means monolithic, however, in their interests, viewpoints, and agendas. For our purposes, we can focus on the strand of the post-Norinaga movement that has probably had the most impact on Shinto—namely, the line of thought associated with Hirata Atsutane (1776–1843). The year 1801 marked not only the death of Norinaga but also the year Atsutane declared himself Norinaga's disciple, even though the two had apparently never met. The interpretation of Shinto developed by Atsutane and his followers, called Hirata Shinto, became an important branch of the more general Fukko Shinto ("returning to the ancient Shinto" or "restoration Shinto") that had been associated with previous Native Studies thinkers, especially Norinaga.

Atsutane's New Vision of Shinto

After an early interest in Chinese classics both Daoist and Confucian, Atsutane turned his focus to Native Studies. Profoundly inspired by Norinaga's writings, he expanded on some of Norinaga's points and marginalized others. Like Norinaga, Atsutane was devoted to Shinto, the ancient way of the *kami.* He was especially taken by Norinaga's concern for uncovering the core of Japaneseness before foreign cultural influences. Not as single-minded as Norinaga in his involvement with philology, Atsutane supplemented his own readings of the ancient texts with an ethnographic study of Japanese folk beliefs and practices. Since Japanese peasants were for the most part not very literate and untouched by either courtly culture or urbanization, Atsutane assumed they had not been hopelessly corrupted by mainland ideas and values. Therefore, he reasoned, if one wanted to recapture the "ancient way" of the Japanese, one could draw on Japanese folk values, ideas, and practices to complement Norinaga's textual studies of the Japanese classics.

At some point, though, Atsutane's project of complementing Norinaga's work became more like *modifying* it. A few issues of divergence will illustrate how Hirata Shinto used Norinaga's ideas as the foundation for a society very different from what Norinaga had imagined as ideal. First, there was a difference in temperament between these two Native Studies scholars. Atsutane did not share Norinaga's pacifist and aesthetic sentiments; he himself had more the personality of a political activist. If Norinaga saw the way to cultural change as a change in heart, Atsutane saw it as a change in will. To take one example of how this difference played out, consider the use of the phrase "*Yamato damashii*" (the spirit of the original Japanese people), a term of central importance to most Native Studies thinkers. To Norinaga it heralded a return to the "feminine" quality of humanity treasured in ancient Japan before the dominance of mainland values. Atsutane, by contrast, related *Yamato damashii* directly to a political slogan of the early nineteenth century: "Revere the emperor; expel the barbarians" *(sonnō jōi)*. The difference between Norinaga and Atsutane, then, is one of aesthetic versus militant engagement with the world.

Second, the methodological differences between the two led to new rules of evidence. On the one hand, we have Norinaga trying to maintain something like an objective philological stance. This position derived from his literalist, almost fundamentalist, respect for the classic texts, especially *Kojiki*. In practice Norinaga was at least as susceptible to eisegesis as any other self-avowed literalist—in reading the text, he inevitably read into it his own point of view. Yet the text—at least methodologically and theoretically—was inviolate. He did not settle in his own view of the ancient way until he could verify that it was also somewhere in the classic texts themselves. On the other hand, we have Atsutane using ethnographic research as an additional basis for evidence and even inspiration. Atsutane did not reject Norinaga's philological methods. Indeed, whenever he could, he made philological, textual arguments to buttress his case. Yet Atsutane's court of appeal was not just *Kojiki* but also the mentality of the rural Japanese peasantry, at least as he understood it. This approach gave Atsutane's accounts an edge of anti-intellectualism and anti-elitism not so visible in Norinaga, despite the latter's railing against the "rationalistic" mentality of the Confucian and Buddhist scholars. For Norinaga, the ancient way needed to be acculturated and learned through an aesthetic community. This is why he preferred the Heian courtly aesthetic to what he considered the undisciplined emotionalism of the earlier *Man'yōshū* poems. These poems, compiled in the eighth century, had been highly prized by Norinaga's Native Studies predecessors since they represented the oldest poems preserved in the Japanese language. Norinaga compared the simple mindful heart of *Man'yōshū* to the purity but plainness of a white kimono, whereas the cultivated mindful heart of the Heian period was a cultured and refined embroidered kimono of courtly elegance. Thus the Heian period's cultivated sensitivity was to him clearly superior to the earlier forms of poetic expression: it was just as sincere as the earlier aesethetic, but it was enriched with a sense of community and tradition. Atsutane, by contrast, thought such cultivated sensitivity reflects foreign influences and insisted it was the uneducated peasants who were most in touch with the ancient Japanese ways.

And third, Atsutane could find in Norinaga's approach assumptions of which the latter had been only vaguely aware—especially assumptions supporting a transition to a more essentialist form of Shinto spirituality. He recognized, above all, that Norinaga's position was built on an essentialist metaphysical premise—namely, there was something unique and spiritually fundamental within the Japanese tradition and its people. On this point Norinaga himself had been somewhat ambivalent. Yes, he believed the Japanese did have something no one else had. But he sometimes attributed that specialness to something other than racial or ethnic superiority. According to Norinaga, for example, the bizarre writing system invented for *Kojiki* did preserve within Japan the uncorrupted creation narrative. Yet he believed that preservation was more a matter of luck, even of poor foresight, on the part of the Japanese rather than spiritual inspiration or racial genius. In short: when it comes to advocating Japanese uniqueness and essentialism, Atsutane's indebtedness to Norinaga does not mean he was completely true to Norinaga's intent.

The relation between ethnic essentialism and universalism is always complex. It seems Norinaga and Atsutane tended to negotiate this relation in slightly different ways. The general issue (by no means limited to the time and place we are discussing here) is how to relate ethnicity (or race or culture) with humanity at large. Suppose we are members of a highly self-conscious and powerful ethnic (or racial or cultural) group. How should "we" understand our relation to those "outside" our group? Consider the following alternatives:

> *Position A:* Our ethnicity (or race or culture) is something true or valuable merely (or primarily) *for us.* Therefore our goal should be to cultivate it locally and not let it be skewed by foreign ideas and values.

> *Position B:* Because of our ethnicity, we have access to something true or valuable *for all humanity,* although others may not yet recognize this. That gives us a responsibility to share what we have with others. There are three options for doing this:

> *Option 1:* We should make every effort to epitomize the paradigm in our own culture in order to exemplify it to the rest of the world. Outsiders can then see for themselves the truth and value our ethnicity or culture represents.

> *Option 2:* We should try to persuade others of the value of our ways by disseminating information and arguing for it openly.

> *Option 3:* For the benefit of others, we should apply some coercion in helping them become more like us. When they later come to understand the superiority of our way of life, they will be grateful for our intervention.

Many Native Studies thinkers, especially before Norinaga, seemed to argue for no more than Position A. They were worried about losing their own cultural and ethnic roots to mainland influences and wanted to excavate and preserve the ancient way of the Japanese before it was lost forever. There is, of course, an element of national pride in such a position, but it need not be imperialistic or even nationalistic. Most of the time Norinaga wrote as though he favored Position A. Yet because he believed he had found the true account for the creation of the world, not just Japan, he also sometimes seemed to hold Position B. That is: because of its distinctive situation, Japanese culture has something in it of value to share with non-Japanese as well. If this is the case, which of the three options for sharing would Norinaga have preferred? Most of the time he seemed to favor Option 1. That is: by establishing an ideal society, the ancient ways preserved and exemplified in Japan could be an inspiration to other peoples. Atsutane, by contrast, seemed most often to favor the interventionism of Options 2 or 3. Certainly the successors in his movement did so. That is: because most Hirata Shinto leaders assumed an essential Japaneseness, it followed that the Japanese would have a unique mission in the world that they were normatively required to pursue. If (as Norinaga claimed) the Japanese have the creation story right and if (as Norinaga often suggested) the creation story applies to the world and not just Japan, then the Japanese emperor has a global, not merely national, role to play. Such was the reasoning in Hirata Shinto.

Based on such differences in perspective and goals, Atsutane's interpretations diverged from Norinaga on two crucial points having a profound effect on the future of Shinto doctrine and its institutionalization: one was the relation between *kami* and creation; the other was the nature of the afterlife. On the surface, these questions would seem rather abstract, arcane metaphysical issues having little to do with nationalism and militarism. In our account, however, we are precisely at that historical point when essentialist Shinto spirituality comes to predominate over existential. In essentialist spiritual traditions, purported essences determine doctrine; doctrine then prescribes or proscribes certain behavior; institutions are then designed to execute these prescriptions and proscriptions. In short: in such a context the development of metaphysical doctrines may be a precursor to major axiological, political, and social change—all in the name of religion or spirituality. Behind the two issues cited here—creation and the afterlife—are key questions that most essentialist traditions tend to address: "how and why are we here?" and "where are we going (or should be going)?"

In answering these two questions, Atsutane argued that one of the *kami* deities mentioned in the ancient chronicles, Amenominakanushi (Ame-no-minaka-nushi), was the single original source of creation. Furthermore, he argued that at the time of death another *kami* deity, Ōkuninushi, would judge the merits of each person's life and determine an appropriate abode in the afterlife. Many scholars, Japanese as well as Western, find intriguing similarities to Christianity in these two views. Since Atsutane had access to at least basic Christian doctrine, the influence is certainly possible. Yet there are ways in which his two views connect with aspects of Buddhism as well. As we have seen, Buddhist-Shinto syncretism had predominated for almost a thousand years. Given the Native Studies agenda to excise all "foreign" elements from Shinto, the internal relation between Buddhism and Shinto was broken. And in any broken internal relation, we have noted, the disconnected components lose part of themselves. Native Studies scholars interested in "restoring" Shinto—people like Atsutane—scrambled to fill in what was missing, something that Buddhism had previously supplied. Furthermore, if Christianity too had some version of this missing part, it was all the more obvious that if Shinto were not to seem inferior or philosophically underdeveloped, it had to address the lack. Let us consider these two issues in more detail so we can explore the intellectual context of Atsutane's enterprise and see why he made the philosophical moves he did.

First there was the matter of creation. If the goal of Native Studies was to go back to the ancient way, then obviously one should go back all the way to the beginning. This was one motive for Norinaga's having spent three decades deciphering *Kojiki,* the earliest text written in the Japanese language. As we have seen, though, if we are to base the Shinto idea of creation on *Kojiki* and *Nihonshoki* accounts alone, there are textual conundrums. Indeed the two accounts blatantly disagree on certain details (such as the birth narrative of the all-important sun *kami*). Textual interpreters could probably in the long run solve this problem, just as biblical commentators have addressed discrepancies between the two creation stories in Genesis, for example. But there was a more serious question, one more metaphysical than textual. The overall thrust in the two Shinto canonical chronicles is that creation often happened fortuitously as an unintended side effect of the gods' activities. In some incidents there might have been some explicit divine intention by this or that *kami,* but there was no clear prevailing divine plan or telos. Furthermore, the textual descriptions were elusive in explaining exactly how the whole process started. The texts relate how various *kami* came into being—but was there a first *kami* and was there anything at all before that *kami*? As we saw in chapter 4, Buddhist-Shinto syncretism had addressed this issue previously through the symbolic correlation of the Sun Goddess (Amaterasu) with the Sun Buddha (the cosmic Dainichi). Although Dainichi did not create the universe, Buddhist doctrine holds that the universe is identical with Dainichi's activity. So everything is at least grounded in Dainichi. Since the *kami* Amaterasu, according to the *honji suijaku* algorithm, is correlated with the buddha Dainichi, she too could be understood as the ontological basis of everything. Certainly this is the implication in the *suijaku* mandala portraying her as the origin of all the *kami*. In excising Buddhism from Shinto, however, the Native Studies scholars could no longer endorse such a theory. There was no canonical basis for it. Indeed, both *Kojiki* and *Nihonshoki* clearly state that other *kami* (including Izanami and Izanagi) preceded Amaterasu. Thus the Buddhist-influenced explanation was not an option and there now was a hole in Shinto cosmogony left by the divorce from Buddhism.

Let us restate this issue as a purely metaphysical problem. Among Shinto's potential competitors—Buddhism, Christianity, and Neo-Confucianism—each maintained a single basis for the nature of reality. Esoteric Buddhism had the Cosmic Buddha, Dainichi; Christianity had the creator God; and Neo-Confucianism had the underlying "pattern" or "principle" (*li* in Chinese; *ri* in Japanese) with which reality is in accord. Shinto, by contrast, at least once severed from Buddhist-Shinto syncretism, lacked a comparable single source for the meaning of creation. Furthermore, when Neo-Confucian–Shinto syncretism developed in the seventeenth century, it encountered the same problem and responded by explaining Shinto ontology through a Neo-Confucian concept. Yamazaki Ansai (1619–1682), for example, in developing his Suika Shinto mentioned in chapter 4, borrowed the Neo-Confucian idea of principle, or pattern, as the underlying source of meaning in reality. Atsutane had as a young man studied under Ansai and was likely well aware of the metaphysical issue at stake. Yet as his own essentialist and nativist form of Shinto developed, Atsutane realized that Shinto needed a distinctively Shinto metaphysical ground, not one borrowed from a foreign tradition, Confucian or Buddhist. What, according to Shinto, was the meaning of it all? Why was there something rather than nothing? What purposive ground was there to reality? Atsutane set out to find it even if this meant deviating from the interpretation of his idol, Norinaga.

Atsutane devised a rereading of a single phrase in the *Kojiki* narrative that allowed him, with some extensive interpretation, to make the claim that indeed there was a beginning to creation and that the creative act was performed by the *kami* deity named Amenominakanushi, the first *kami* named in the narrative. This newly devised Shinto cosmogonic doctrine presented a viable native alternative to the metaphysical basis of meaning derived from Buddhism, Neo-Confucianism, or Christianity. For Atsutane, the world is not an extension of the Sun Buddha's cosmic body; it is not a process according with a pattern or principle as maintained in Neo-Confucianism; it is not the creation of the Christian God. Instead it is the willful act of a creator *kami*: Amenominakanushi. Atsutane maintained this to be a purely Shinto doctrine grounded in canonical texts.

At first glance, it might seem strange that Atsutane would develop an interpretation that seemed to lower the status of the Sun Goddess. After all, Atsutane was a staunch supporter of reinstating true imperial rule and Amaterasu was the source of imperial kinship and charismatic authority. Yet in Atsutane's account, not Amaterasu but Amenominakanushi was ontologically the most fundamental *kami*. Although this claim might seem counterproductive to Atsutane's hope to reestablish imperial rule, consider the trade-off. His account divorced Amaterasu's connection with the Sun Buddha. She had attained her cosmological priority in Buddhist-Shinto syncretism only as a "trace manifestation" of the Cosmic Buddha, Dainichi. No one could ever claim with a straight face that either *Kojiki* or *Nihonshoki* had granted her that status. Before the Buddhist-Shinto syncretism, her special standing resided in the belief that her rule over this earthly realm (or, depending on the interpretation, over the land of Japan) had been delegated by the other celestial *kami*. According to the myths in the two chronicles, Amaterasu had relatively little to do with the creation of the world. Yet so long as one granted that all the *kami* had given Amaterasu dominion over this world, the imperial throne would by extension still have its charismatic authority. After all, the emperor does not reign over the universe, but only this earthly realm or this land of Japan. From Atsutane's vantage point, he had uncovered a single origin and a divine plan that ran from creation, through the *kami* deities who gave Amaterasu rule over this world, through Amaterasu, and directly to the Japanese imperial succession. Through Atsutane's doctrinal maneuver, the internal relation between imperial rule and the *kami* still traces back to creation itself and there is no recourse to any doctrines from traditions outside Shinto. There would no longer be any need, indeed no possibility, of syncretizing Shinto with the cosmogonic metaphysics of any other religion. If Atsutane's new interpretation meant that Amaterasu could no longer be viewed as the ontological basis of reality, he could accept that. The important issue for him was that through his new Shinto cosmogony he had sealed off the Shinto essence from violation by any foreign elements and had maintained, even strengthened, the distinctively Shinto justification for imperial rule.

Let us turn now to Atsutane's second major modification of Norinaga's Shinto legacy: his reinterpretation of the afterlife. Based on his reading of *Kojiki,* as we have seen, Norinaga had believed in the dark underworld of decomposing corpses: the Land of Yomi. Such a view was all that Norinaga could justify through his textual studies, and his methodological rigor committed him to saying nothing further. Given his instructions to his disciples about his own burial, Norinaga seems to have held this view throughout his life. But, we recall, Atsutane had additional sources to guide his thinking on such issues: the folk beliefs of the ordinary people. At the popular level, we have already seen how complex and multilayered is the Japanese view of what happens after death—affording Atsutane considerable space within which to construct his theory. Without going into detail about his evidence, we can just consider the gist of his idea. In reading the *Kojiki* and *Nihonshoki* accounts, Atsutane chose to underscore a polarity between good and evil in addition to the usual Shinto emphasis on pollution and purification. Such a moral binary was quite alien to Norinaga, who regarded moralizing as indicative of the disparaged "Chinese mentality." Atsutane's reading, however, allowed him to establish a *kami*-based foundation for good and bad behavior: to follow the way of the *kami* was good; to deviate, evil. Furthermore, he put forward the idea that at the time of death one's future destiny would be determined by the life one had led. That is: disagreeing with Norinaga, Atsutane did not maintain that the Land of Yomi was the eternal abode for everyone who died. How people live and die makes a difference for their fate in the afterlife.

Norinaga's insistence on the Land of Yomi account had been based squarely on his reading of *Kojiki* and nothing else. In fact, as we have seen, Norinaga's pacifism was based in part on his belief that there was nothing positive about death and its sequel. In the popular Japanese belief systems of the time, however, the Land of Yomi had little prominence and Atsutane's view of the afterlife resonated better with the assumptions of most Japanese. After all, Buddhism had always maintained that one's rebirth after death would be determined by how one had led one's life—a consequence of Buddhism's general theory of karma. Many schools of Buddhism, including the popular Japanese Pure Land traditions, had focused on the ideal abode into which one could be reborn after this lifetime. Certainly Buddhist funeral rites of any sort (and by this time almost all funerals were Buddhist) would have reinforced this idea further. Moreover, even in the Shinto-related traditions we have noted the example of Michizane, who became after death a "heavenly *kami*" *(tenjin)*. Add further the strongly entrenched belief in ghosts and spirits among the Japanese. Collectively these factors contributed to the Japanese tendency to accept Atsutane's differentiated view of the afterlife as a site of reward and punishment.

Did Atsutane's Shinto interpretation of the afterlife make any practical difference? It certainly did. Consider the consequences if Norinaga's Land of Yomi interpretation had prevailed. Based on that view, no matter what one did in this life, one's fate after death was the same: continued decay in the putrid underworld. For Norinaga there was no upside to death. Death is for us humans a bad thing and one can only be resigned to it, never finding any consolation in it. Shinto for him was the celebration of life: its precious evanescence, its participation in wonder, its resonance among the *kokoro* of human beings, things, and words. Such was Shinto for the pacifist aesthete. On the other side we have Atsutane. How one lives one's life, whether in accord with the *kami* or against the *kami,* has great consequences at the time of death. To die in defense of the emperor, for example, would be to live in accord with the design of the world from the time of its creation. There would have to be a reward in the afterlife for such dedication to the ancient *kami* way. As we have noted, Atsutane explained the *Yamato damashii,* the "spirit of the original Japanese," in terms of the slogan "Revere the emperor; expel the barbarians." Thus to die for the emperor, he believed, could not mean going to some underworld of great defilement. Quite the contrary, Ōkuninushi would judge such a person good and reward the soul accordingly in the afterlife. Such was a Shinto view of death befitting a militarist like Atsutane.

In chapter 3 we saw that one could have constructed an argument for an essentialist Shinto based on eighth-century assumptions. The hypothetical argument to a Japanese audience went like this:

> As explained in *Nihonshoki* and *Kojiki,* you are indebted to the *kami* deities for your personal existence and the existence of your world. Given this dependence, you are internally related to the *kami* deities. The emperors and empresses are the direct descendants of these *kami,* and given their special role it is through them you contact your link with the *kami.* Therefore, if you are Japanese, you must be Shinto; if you are Shinto, you owe absolute allegiance to the emperors or empresses and to the government serving them.

No one in the eighth century made this argument explicitly, of course, but the seeds were all there. Chapter 4 explained how Buddhist-Shinto syncretism delayed their germination. When he found the seeds while tilling his native soil, Norinaga thought them the seeds that flowered last and most brilliantly in Heian culture. Atsutane, however, saw them as the seeds of revolution. He made explicit the Native Studies ideology for an essentialist Shinto spirituality—an ideology hidden for a thousand years—and replanted the seeds so that they bore fruit as a full-grown essentialist Shinto spirituality that would nourish a new vision of the Japanese state.

To sum up: by the early decades of the nineteenth century, in developing its theory of Fukko (Restoration) Shinto based on a revival and reconstruction of certain eighth-century ideas, the Native Studies movement had put in place an ideology lending Shinto a set of distinct characteristics. First, it now (thanks to Norinaga) had an official canon—*Nihonshoki* and, most especially, *Kojiki*. Second, a nostalgic, romanticized view of the past developed around the idea that there was something essentially special and distinctive about being Japanese—and this essence was intricately intertwined with Shinto. Third, Shinto doctrine, including its cosmogony and metaphysical ground, had been hermetically sealed off from other spiritual traditions—most critically, the intimacy between Buddhist and Shinto doctrine was broken. Fourth, the argument for the centrality of the emperor was reaffirmed and reinforced by making him the holograph of the Japanese people, the land, and the *kami*. Fifth, Atsutane's particular form of Restoration Shinto added a bipolar analysis of good and evil—fully developed with implications for the afterlife. Collectively these characteristics became the philosophical underpinnings for a new essentialist Shinto spirituality: Shinto had a unique core distinguishing it from all other religions, an emergent doctrinal system upon which to base normative arguments, and an explicit justification for a new institutional structure (based on imperial rule) that would be the foundation for centralized oversight of behavior, ideas, and values. Philosophically at least, Shinto identity was no longer an ex post facto description of how someone feels and acts. It had now become the essence of being Japanese—an essence with clear normative prescriptions about how one *should* act, think, and feel.

Let us not be too idealistic about how change really happens, though. Both Hegel and the popular idiom are wrong: ideas do not change the world; people with ideas change the world. In fact, change usually requires *lots* of people working together even though they may not share identical ideas or values. This is why, after a successful revolution, the question of "now what?" is often so divisive among the victors. While they may have agreed on the pragmatic question of what should no longer continue, after the revolution they may discover profound disagreements over what should be put in its stead. In the end, Atsutane was not the right person for the job of transforming the Japanese state. He was an intellectual with only the most modest political and economic base. In fact, in his final years, when it appeared that he might be starting to attract a significant number of followers, the shogun banished him to the northernmost regions of the country. In the decades after the restoration of the emperor in 1868, however, the victors' histories valorized Atsutane as a hero of imperial nationalism and "Hirata Shinto" became, at least for a time, a label of official adulation. In short: Hirata Shinto had less ideological influence on the revolution than it was to have in the decades afterward.

The Restoration of Imperial Rule

If not Atsutane, who then were the agents of change? Three groups stand out as major players: intellectuals, peasants, and samurai domain lords. In the first group were those intellectuals who did have access to money, prestige, and political power. The call for the restoration of the emperor to political authority was not limited to the Native Studies thinkers, however. Also involved were groups of Confucian thinkers, especially those in a Confucian-Shinto alliance to support the emperor. Such groups often had more political resources than the upstart Native Studies scholars. The most influential was probably the Mito school, a Confucian and later Confucian-Shinto think tank centered in the domain of Mito not far from Edo (Tokyo). This school originated as a project to write a comprehensive history of Japan's imperial dynasty. The founding patron of the project was Tokugawa Mitsukuni (1661–1690), grandson of the first Tokugawa shogun, Ieyasu. By the late eighteenth century, the Mito school had become a hotbed of nationalistic pride and loyalty to the emperor. In fact, Aizawa Seishisai (1782–1863), a scholar in service to the Mito lord, Tokugawa Nariaki (1800–1860), seems to have been the first to come up with the four-character motto we have mentioned in relation to Atsutane: sonnō jōi, "Revere the emperor; expel the barbarians." Through an ironic chain of events, Nariaki's son, Tokugawa Yoshinobu (1837–1913), was the sitting shogun during the Meiji Restoration in 1868 and had to surrender his power to the emperor. This suggests how close the Mito school scholars were to power—both power that was and power that could be. With such intricate connections to authority, the Mito school intellectuals obviously had a larger role than the Hirata nativists in the power politics of the restoration. Yet because the Mito school was more concerned with historical studies and politics than religion, once the restoration was complete the Hirata version of Shinto was poised to exert its influence. (The intellectuals behind the imperial restoration government were so out of touch with Native Studies, incidentally, that they had assumed Norinaga's and Atsutane's views of Shinto were identical. It took two or three decades to sort out the differences and, as it was clarified, Hirata Shinto gradually lost much of its cachet.)

The peasants comprised the second group of agents actively involved in the Meiji Restoration. In their two and half centuries of rule, the Tokugawa shoguns and the domain lords they supported had established severe policies of taxation and had manipulated the rice market, creating devastating hardship on the farmers. In response, there were sporadic peasant uprisings throughout the Tokugawa era. In the prerestoration years of the nineteenth century we sometimes find a potent alliance between intellectuals and farmers in these uprisings. During the famine of 1837, for example, there were two notable peasant revolts. The one in Osaka was led by a Neo-Confucian scholar named Ōshio Heihachirō (1793–1837). In the end, the leader had to commit suicide when the uprising failed—but only after the rebellion had destroyed about one-fourth of the buildings in Osaka. The other was an uprising in what is now Niigata prefecture led by Ikuta Yorozu (1801–1837), a student of Atsutane. In this case, Atsutane's nonelitist contacts with the Japanese peasantry did have a concrete political outcome. Ikuta, the founder of a local Native Studies school, had repeatedly complained to the local lord about extortionate rice prices. In desperation he led a failed rebellion and, like Ōshio, eventually had to commit suicide.

The third group of agents of change were the various domain lords from around Japan who had strong loyalties to the emperor. Like the peasants, many lords had multiple grievances against the shogunate over the centuries. Furthermore, many of the more militant samurai lords disagreed with shogunate policies toward the threat of Western imperialism. From early in the nineteenth century, Western ships had haphazardly ended up in Japanese waters or even come ashore. The militarist lords of various domains saw this as an imminent threat and found the shogunate impotent in taking the countermeasures they felt essential to Japan's defense. As indicated by the peasant uprisings, the shogunate was clearly losing its tight-fisted control over internal affairs. Now there was an even more ominous threat from abroad. When Commodore Matthew Perry's gunboats entered Tokyo harbor in 1853 and 1854, forcing Japan to open itself to trade with the United States, many domain lords saw this as the final, unacceptable capitulation to outside imperialist powers. The collective pressure of various groups caused the Tokugawa shogun Yoshinobu to turn over most of his power to the emperor. This last-ditch attempt to save at least the vestige of the shogunate office failed when a group of samurai led by lords from the southern provinces of Satsuma (today Kagoshima) and Chōshū (today Yamaguchi) took the imperial palace in Kyoto by storm, eventually forcing the complete abdication of the Tokugawa shogunate's powers. The capital (the residence city of the emperor) moved from Kyoto to Edo, henceforth called "Tokyo" (Eastern Capital).

Let us sum up these conditions leading to the Meiji Restoration. The three key groups—intellectuals, peasants, and samurai domain lords—collaborated in creating the intellectual, popular, and military support needed to overthrow the shogunate. All three groups had connections with Shinto either directly, as in Hirata Shinto's influence in the Ikuta Yorozu Uprising, or indirectly through their allegiance to the emperor as the true ruler of Japan. Since the authority of that imperial rule was now ideologically entrenched in Restoration Shinto ideology, it was natural that Shinto would play a key role in the new imperial government. In this enterprise, at least initially, Hirata Shinto would be paramount.

Modern Shinto During the War Years (1894–1945)

Between the years 1894 (the beginning of the Sino-Japanese War) through 1945 (the end of World War II), Japan was either at war someplace abroad or retooling for the next such war. Never before had Japan gone to war for any sustained period outside the boundaries of its own country. So "foreign war" was a relatively new Japanese phenomenon calling for internal analysis and interpretation. The newly developing essentialist Shinto ideology was pivotal in this project. To define an ideological space for enlisting essentialist Shinto spirituality in the service of nationalism, the Japanese government supported what is usually called today "State Shinto." The emergence of State Shinto cannot be defined as a single event; rather, it was a complex process starting at the dawn of the Meiji period in 1868 and extending to the end of the Pacific War in 1945. The very term "State Shinto," in fact, has become common mainly since 1945. Only recently have hindsight and academic freedom allowed scholars to examine critically the relation between Shinto and the modern Japanese state.

State Shinto is not an institution but an ideology deriving many of its basic concepts from the analyses developed by Hirata Shinto and the Mito school. Its driving idea is that the Japanese state is centered in the emperor. Indeed in 1868, almost as soon as the Meiji Restoration had succeeded, the government officially called for the "oneness of [Shinto] ritual and political administration." This declaration harks back to the original link between *matsuri* and *matsurigoto* discussed in chapter 2. Once again, in new terms and new contexts, the affirmation was that the emperor is Japan's holographic entry point reflecting the mysterious, *tama*-energized whole. This whole includes the emperor's intimate connectedness with the celestial *kami* of creation, the land of Japan, the ethnicity of the Japanese people, the governance of the state, and more. Because the emperor is the holographic entry point for being Japanese, the essentialist ideology maintains that a person cannot fathom one's own Japaneseness or act Japanese without going through this entry point. In short: because of the imperial connection to Amaterasu, the emperor is the sine qua non of the Japanese state. If one does not pass through this holographic entry point to be connected with the whole, one cannot by definition be patriotic, genuine, sincere, or fully energized with *tama*. One's very spirit or soul *(mitama* or *tamashii)* will be incomplete without this holographic relation with imperial charisma. Note the essentialist nature of this ideology. In this new context, "Shinto" is not the name for a description of how people act, think, and feel. Instead it is the name for an essential quality that prescribes, rather than describes, proper conduct.

Ideologies are no more than abstract concepts, however, until they assume institutional reality. Although "State Shinto" technically never existed as an institution itself, as an ideology it did drive the abolition and creation of several institutions. The new government in the latter part of the nineteenth century had three reorganizational strategies related to Shinto. Two of these were institutional dismantlings; the third was a new structure. First, following what the Native Studies thinkers had already done philosophically, the government proceeded to dissolve the institutional overlaps of Shinto with Buddhism. Although many Japanese thinkers had been separating out "native" spirituality from Buddhism for several decades, the everyday practice of religion in Japan had continued to be synergistic. Furthermore, as mentioned earlier, a number of shrines, such as those of the Ryōbu tradition, were in Buddhist precincts and overseen by Buddhist priests. In 1869 the newly established imperial government forced a separation between the two traditions: Shinto precincts within former Buddhist complexes had to be walled off into separate compounds containing no images or structures related to Buddhism; only Shinto priests could head a shrine; government support of Buddhist temples ended. For a few years there were even sporadic local proscriptions against Buddhism—going so far as to require the removal of Buddhist images from homes.

The Japanese government's second deconstructive activity was to remove from Shinto any residual texts, doctrines, groups, and practices that did not fit cleanly the ideology of State Shinto. Some of these were Shinto-related religious groups like Tenrikyō and Kurozumikyō that had arisen only in the nineteenth century, basing their ideas, values, and practices on a charismatic founder's revelatory experience. Others were Shinto institutions with a long history of independent doctrinal development such as the Yoshida and Watarai (Ise) shrine groups cited earlier. Starting in 1876, the government began granting such Shinto groups the official designation of "Sect Shinto." By 1908 the number of Sect Shinto groups had risen to its maximum of thirteen. The advantage of the "Sect Shinto" designation derived from the newly recognized right to religious freedom guaranteed in the 1889 Meiji Constitution. By being officially designated a religious sect, the new groups of Sect Shinto would, like Christianity, be "religions" (shūkyō) protected from any official government interference in their teachings and practices. Of course, the other side of the coin was that designation as a "religion" also precluded any government financial support for the groups.

As the ideology of State Shinto became increasingly entrenched, however, some sects under the Sect Shinto umbrella discovered how qualified their constitutionally protected religious freedom could be. The logic of the State Shinto ideology stipulated that any actions, values, or ideas not in line with its principles were unpatriotic or even treasonable. That is: Japanese citizens were free to practice any religion they wished; but if they did not accept and act in accordance with State Shinto ideology, they were traitors who could be imprisoned or executed. This is exactly what happened to some Sect Shinto leaders.

Obviously there was a discrepancy between the rhetoric of religious freedom and the persecution of those who did not follow the State Shinto ideology. One could easily assume that the persecutions were simply illegal—that the government officials were blatantly disregarding Japan's own laws. Arguably they violated the spirit of the law (at least in terms of how the West understood the idea of religious freedom), but they may not have violated its letter. The inclusion of religious freedom in the Meiji Constitution of 1889 was partly to appease Western insistence that there be no persecution of Christianity in Japan. Thus the Westerners were satisfied. By 1905, however, Japan had proved itself a mighty imperialist nation in its own right, having defeated China and Russia in separate wars. It no longer had to kowtow to every Western imperialist demand. In return, the Western nations, when they worried about Japan at all instead of their own military and economic problems elsewhere in the world, focused on matters more important to them than the Japanese citizen's right to practice religion freely.

Left to their own devices, the Japanese police and prosecutors found it rather easy to frame religious dissent not as exercising religious freedom protected in the constitution, but as violating the same constitution's affirmations about the "sacred and inviolate nature" of the emperor and his explicit right to govern without disloyalty. The government at times insisted that even Christian and Buddhist clergy affirm in their sermons the sanctity of the emperor and the protecting power of the *kami*. This brings us to the government's constructive rather than dismantling activities in institutionalizing the State Shinto ideology.

As we have seen, right from the start the postrestoration government had sought to disentangle Shinto from both "alien" Buddhist elements and Shinto-related groups that might be internal irritants to the establishment of the state ideology. After these exclusions, there remained the vast majority of the Shinto shrines: the great national shrines, many pilgrimage sites, most regional centers for festivals, even village agrarian shrines dedicated to tutelary *kami*. Although these shrines were impressive in their collective numbers (over 100,000), they were in a weak position on several fronts. First, having lost the generally well-educated Buddhist priests who had formally headed many of the larger shrines, there was a dearth of skilled Shinto leadership to fill the vacuum. Second, however numerous, the various shrines were generally not well integrated into any organizational system or network. And third, given their regional differences in praxis and even doctrine, there was no clear practical or philosophical basis for unifying them. Given this weakness, the State Shinto leaders first tried to develop a national spirituality—not a religion *(shūkyō)*—that was independent and transcendent to either Buddhism or Shinto. They tried to set up such a system of "National Teachings" to be taught by approved priests, whether Shinto or Buddhist in background, trained in a state-sponsored national institution. For various reasons, the idea failed. But the leaders of Ise shrine (dedicated to the sun *kami*) volunteered to pick up the program and have it centered there at Ise instead of Tokyo. This led to a new institutional strategy.

Rather than establishing a new spiritual, but not "religious," institution to support the state, now the strategy was to use the shrines existing throughout Japan. Given their institutional weakness, they were ripe for reorganization. Torn from their previous linkages, they had lost the sophistication of Buddhist doctrine and the vitality of the new religions cropping up in the nineteenth century. Until the nineteenth century, people generally did not worry about whether they were practicing Buddhism or Shinto since their syncretistic union had made them so interdependent in their worldviews. By disengaging them in 1869, however, each of the related pair, both Shinto and Buddhism, lost part of itself. Because of their strong internal relations forged over the previous millennium, Shinto could not go back to being just Shinto; nor could Buddhism return to being just Buddhism. Why not, figured the nationalists, simply graft the State Shinto ideology and praxis onto the Shinto shrines to replace the hole left by Buddhism? This is exactly what the government did. It called its new official institution "Shrine Shinto."

The government insisted that Shrine Shinto, unlike Sect Shinto, was not a religion. Therefore the state could support it: giving the financially strapped shrines and their priests significant financial resources; overseeing Shrine Shinto's doctrinal development in a new, government-sponsored educational system for Shinto priests; establishing civil rites at existing shrines all over Japan and at any new ones the government decided to build; organizing these shrines into a single system easily supervised by government bureaucracies; teaching Shrine Shinto's "nonreligious" ideology in schools; demanding that all Japanese citizens believe in it and participate in its practices (forcing family registration at Shinto shrines instead of Buddhist temples, for example). The abstract ideology of State Shinto had found its ideal concrete institutional form: Shrine Shinto.

Let us examine the claim that Shrine Shinto was not religious. It could be argued that it was not religious in the way Sect Shinto, Christianity, and Buddhism were. To affiliate with these groups was a matter of choice for the Japanese citizen. Shrine Shinto, by contrast, was simply a responsibility of citizenship as fundamental as allegiance to the national flag. Yet Shrine Shinto, with its most important rituals presided over by the emperor, the chief priest of Shinto, was not exactly irreligious either. It was certainly "spiritual," not only in its praxes, but also in its use of terms like *"tama," "tamashii," "mitama,"* and *"kami."* By this maneuver the nationalist/militarist ideologues had secured a way of being able to define Shrine Shinto as either spiritual or civil, according to their needs, but all along being able to maintain it was not a religion. (Here the ambiguities of the Japanese *"shūkyō"* discussed in chapter 1 are particularly relevant.) The "nonreligious" designation of Shrine Shinto also legally entitled the state to use Shinto however it wanted in its educational system and official state propaganda. The Imperial Rescript on Education of 1890 epitomized the exercise of this power—developing the guiding principles about the sacred status of the throne and the necessity of always displaying loyalty and filial piety in relation to the emperor.

Consequently, besides the reasons discussed in chapter 1, we now have another reason many Japanese find it comfortable today to say they are "not religious" even though they may participate regularly in various rituals (some Shinto in pedigree). For half a century, in schools and in public rhetoric, the Japanese were taught that one does not have to be "religious" to hold beliefs or engage in practices related to *kami, tama, mitama,* and *tamashii.* Nor need there be anything "religious," they were taught, about revering the emperor or finding sacredness in the natural phenomena of Japan. According to the official ideology arising in the late nineteenth century, to say one is "Shinto" means by definition that one is "not religious" (unless one is a member of one of the small number of Sect Shinto groups). From this standpoint there is no contradiction in saying, for example, "I am not religious" and "I worship a fox at least once a year" or even "I am Shinto but not religious." Clearly the legacy of this state ideology still influences Japanese statements of self-identification in surveys of the kind discussed in chapter 1.

Through such legalistic and institutional strategies, the establishment of essentialist Shinto spirituality was complete. Shrine Shinto affirmed a national quintessence for the Japanese—a spiritual essence even more fundamental than any "religion." To criticize this essence was itself proof that one was not of the "body [or essence] of our (Japanese) state," the literal meaning of *"kokutai."* Originally emphasized by the Mito school thinkers, *"kokutai"* became a favored term among political thinkers during the foreign war years. The term referred (in an appropriately holographic way) to both the empire and the emperor. Loyalty to the emperor was not a choice but a recognition and expression of one's own Japaneseness. To deny the *kokutai* would mean that one is not part of the holograph, not part of all the internal, intimate relations defining what it means to be Japanese. Dissent was, in effect, a suicidal act upon one's own identity.

It has become commonplace, incidentally, to translate *"kokutai"* into English as "national polity," but this rendering is linguistically and philosophically inappropriate. Linguistically one can say in English that virtually every civilized country has some kind of "national polity," but in Japanese *"kokutai"* applies specifically to the purportedly unique form of Japan's political/spiritual/imperial structure. In fact, technically speaking, *kokutai* is not a political structure at all but a metaphysical ideology legitimating a certain form of polity. Furthermore, it is linguistically peculiar to translate *"kokutai"* as "polity" when the word "polity" is not translated into Japanese as *"kokutai"* unless it is applying specifically and uniquely to Japan. And philosophically there is the history of the idea of polity itself in the West going back through medieval thought to the ancient Greeks. In this intellectual development, the Western assumption has usually been that people or societies fashion their particular polity. The Japanese idea, by contrast, is that the organization is a sacred unit going back to the time of creation, a unit that resonates affectively, intellectually, and uniquely in the soul of every Japanese. In this respect, to translate *"kokutai"* simply as "national polity" is to despiritualize, obscure, and defang the distinctive force of the Japanese term.

In short: by the early twentieth century it had become virtually impossible to undermine the state ideology and its institutional support from within. To impugn the State Shinto ideology could only indicate one was not part of the *kokutai*. To criticize the ideology meant that, by definition, one was "not Japanese," that one had denied one's own essence. Therefore, the criticism could not be sincere *(makoto)*. Ultimately a successful attack on the ideology had to come from outside: only the defeat of Japan itself could prove the ideology a sham. Despite the power of the *kami* of the winds (kamikaze) holographically centered in brave pilots who flew into the rising sun to their deaths, despite the pure mindful hearts of the Japanese people resonating in the mystery of the *kokutai*, the militarist regime and its ideology did fail. In fact, in August 1945 it was shown that even a strictly material force could defeat the false spiritual-material ideology. The Americans had put their trust in a machine of fire, not the deity of the winds. And the Americans had won.

Shinto Since 1945

With General MacArthur's occupation forces in the wings, the emperor formally and publicly announced on January 1, 1946, that he was not divine. He said that the relation between the emperor and the people was not based on "mere legends and myths" (such as those of *Kojiki*), but on the consent of the people, and that it was "false" that the "emperor is divine and that the Japanese people are superior to other races." Within a few years, the Supreme Commander for the

Allied Powers (SCAP) and his offices successfully dismantled most Shrine Shinto institutions and bureaucracies. But Shrine Shinto, as we have seen, was only an institutionalization of State Shinto. What about the ideology itself? It had obviously been drilled into three or four generations of Japanese schoolchildren. Could SCAP dismantle its values, ideas, and behavior as readily it could its institutions? Let us consider a complex of issues revolving around a single site of contention: Yasukuni shrine in Tokyo.

Imagine this scene from late summer 2001. A group of South Korean males in their twenties are taking part in a political demonstration in their home country. They call themselves the "Save the

Yasukuni Shrine
The front of the shrine building where people come to venerate the spirits of those who have died in service to the emperor.

Nation Squad." At the appointed time, a few kneel on the ground with a butcher's block and knife in front of them. To express the sincerity and intensity of his protest, each young man proceeds to cut off the tip of his little finger with the knife. What are they protesting? That on August 13, 2001, Koizumi Jun'ichirō had made an official visit to Yasukuni shrine in Tokyo and signed the register with not only his name but also his title, "Prime Minister of Japan." This protest was only the most grisly of a flurry of demonstrations from countries victimized by the Japanese in the 1930s and 1940s. The most official and vociferous condemnations came from China and South Korea, but there were strongly worded criticisms from the Philippines as well and various countries in Southeast Asia. Many Japanese, too, lodged their dissent in a variety of venues: newspaper editorials, letters to the editor, student demonstrations, articles by intellectuals in magazines, and so forth. The criticism was so strong, in fact, that many doubted Koizumi would again make an official visit. But he did—in April 2002. Again the protests were sounded. Two Japanese groups combined to bring a class action suit against the government, Koizumi, and the shrine. The eighty-seven plaintiffs consisted mainly of relatives of deceased servicemen whose ashes are entombed at Yasukuni. The suit argues that the prime minister's official visit was a violation of the constitution's separation of church and state. The suit seeks a restraining order against future visits by the prime minister and asks for token compensation (less than $100) to each complainant.

How does a single Shinto shrine find itself so embroiled in both national and international controversy? The situation can be analyzed from various perspectives. Here we will use the events of Yasukuni as a case study for understanding some unresolved conflicts between existential and essentialist elements of Shinto. We have often noted a Shinto shrine can be a holographic entry point. In this case, to pass through the *torii* at Yasukuni today is to reflect the whole of Shinto history over the past two centuries. To analyze Yasukuni will not only bring us up to date in our analysis of Shinto, but it will also allow us to review the major points of this chapter.

First, however, we need to sketch the history of the shrine. Yasukuni (Pacifying Our Country) shrine stands across the street from the imperial palace in the Kudan section of Tokyo. It was built in 1869 under the name "Shōkonsha" (Shrine for Beckoning the Spirits), but in 1879 it was given its present name as it assumed its status as a central shrine with various branch *shōkonsha* established throughout the country. These *shōkonsha*, of which Yasukuni is the prototype (and in effect the holographic entry point for all of them), were built to enshrine the spirits of the Japanese who died for their emperor in either the Meiji Restoration civil war or in the ensuing foreign wars. In other words: Yasukuni basically enshrines those who "died for the emperor" from 1853 (the date Perry entered Tokyo Bay) up through the end of the Pacific War. Altogether there are some 2.5 million enshrined there (all individually named and almost always including their funerary ashes).

As we have noted, until the late nineteenth century Japan had virtually no experience in fighting international wars. Hence, in some ways, the very idea of military personnel who had "died for their country" or, specifically, "died for their emperor" was a new one. How should the state treat the remains and the "souls" *(mitama or tamashii)* of such heroes? Following Atsutane's interpretation, the assumption was that such souls would be greatly rewarded in the afterlife. In dying for the emperor, they had achieved the fullest act of self-realization. They had passed through the holographic entry point and now, somehow, reflect the whole of the protecting spirit of Japan. If, as Atsutane had proclaimed, "to revere the emperor and expel the barbarian" was the true meaning of the "spirit of ancient Japan," then in dying for the emperor the soul of the individual somehow merged into the sacred whole. The establishment of Yasukuni shrine gave this idea a concrete institutional expression.

To understand exactly what happens when a spirit is enshrined at Yasukuni, we need to understand one way in which the Japanese have understood the relation between the individual and the souls of ancestors. Perhaps this understanding is most explicitly expressed in the rituals of the funeral of an emperor and the coronation of his successor. The spirit *(mitama or tamashii)* of the deceased emperor leaves the body and ultimately rejoins the collective imperial *tama.* This pool of *tama* is probably most easily thought of as a living force directly linked to the *kami,* especially Amaterasu. At the coronation the *tama* is sent into the new emperor, energizing his own individual spirit. Technically it is through this *tama* transference that the emperor becomes *kami*. Some Japanese throughout history have understood a similar dynamic between themselves and their own ancestral *tama*. Although the theoretical understanding is probably not as clear as the doctrines behind the imperial succession, the general understanding is that upon death the individual spirit (at least in part) merges into the family's ancestral spirit and subsequently the accumulated ancestral spirit becomes a kind of tutelary power for the family. That is: as time passes after death, one's spirit is less individuated and more part of the ancestral whole. (This idea probably goes back to the ancient idea of the *uji-gami* discussed in chapter 3.) Now let us see how this thinking applies to the understanding of what happens at Yasukuni.

To be enshrined at Yasukuni is to be *kami*. Hence all those who have "died for the emperor" during the foreign war years, almost 2.5 million souls *(mitama)*, are now *kami*. In dying for the emperor, they have realized most fully their own *tama* nature; they have expressed their spiritual essence in its purest form. In so dying, they have holographically reflected the holistic *tama* of the emperor, the land of Japan, and its people. So when one is enshrined at Yasukuni, one's individuated *tama* has merged into a collective *tama* protecting and energizing all Japan. During the foreign war years, new recruits were brought to Yasukuni to undergo a ritual for receiving the *tama* of the *kami* warriors who had gone before in the supreme act of self-realization. We can see the parallel here with the ritual of imperial succession. By receiving the ancestral *tama*, the emperor becomes *kami*. Similarly, because they have become *kami*, the collective *tama* of those who have gone to war previously now energizes and spiritualizes those who are about to go to war next. Hence the very institution and history of Yasukuni closely link Shinto ritual, State Shinto ideology, and Japanese militarism.

The situation is further complicated by the question of who qualifies for enshrinement. There are two aspects to this issue. Both have triggered controversy in Japan and abroad alike. First, all military personnel who died in service to the emperor during the foreign war years belong there. It is as if the collective *tama* requires every individual *mitama* to merge with it. If the remains of a Japanese soldier who died in 1944 were discovered today in, say, the Philippines, the Japanese government would act to enshrine the name and ashes of that soldier in Yasukuni shrine—regardless of the desires of the deceased's family. Legal battles have ensued over such issues. The second complicating factor is that "those who have died for the emperor" include, in the government's interpretation, even those responsible for war atrocities. Those executed in the war crime trials following the Japanese surrender, for example, are also enshrined at Yasukuni. That the Japanese would consider such people *kami* and that the prime minister of Japan would make an official visit to the site granting them this status is particularly offensive to those victimized by the Japanese during the war years.

In fact, Koizumi was not the only prime minister to visit Yasukuni. There were unofficial visits in the early 1950s, too, but they were discontinued because of public outcry in both Japan and abroad. So it was major news when Prime Minister Nakasone Yasuhiro made an "official" visit to the shrine on August 15, 1985, the fortieth anniversary of Japan's official surrender in World War II. Nakasone's visit to Yasukuni shrine spurred a national and international uproar. Asian countries like China and South Korea sent official protests to the Japanese government. Within Japan itself, the right wing vehemently defended Nakasone's act while the left just as vociferously denounced it. The turmoil was such that Nakasone did not return. In 1996 Prime Minister Hashimoto Ryūtarō did make a "personal, not official" visit to the shrine. He made a point of visiting in July, and not on August 15, to avoid direct connections with Nakasone's official visit. In 2001 Koizumi, who had made a campaign promise to visit the shrine if elected, avoided the August 15 date by showing up two days earlier than expected. He signed the register with his title, "Prime Minister of Japan," but did not follow precisely the regimen of a religious visit (placing flowers instead of the *sakaki* branches, for example). His 2002 visit, as noted, was in April, although some of his ministers did visit again on August 15, 2002.

The Japanese government has tried to justify its activities related to Yasukuni in various ways. First, it has rerun State Shinto's old "not a religion" argument. Koizumi's tactic in not following the religiously ritualistic regimen is just one example of this strategy. The tactic was an attempt to avoid the constitutional issue of the separation of religion and state. Second, the government has noted that Japan lacks the equivalent of a military burial ground such as Arlington National Cemetery in the United States. Thus to honor officially those who have died for their country—which virtually every modern nation does—there is no alternative to Yasukuni. (At times the government has entertained the idea of building such a cemetery as a way of alleviating the political problems surrounding Yasukuni, but there has not been much of a concrete plan along these lines.) And third, it is a distinctive honor to have one's relative enshrined as a *kami*. (Theoretically the family's ancestral *tama* gets directly linked somehow to the imperial *tama* through the ritualized enshrinement at Yasukuni.) To change the present status of those spirits of the dead by deconstructing Yasukuni, it is argued, would in some way be a horrible offense to millions of Japanese.

As much as the government has tried to finesse the issues, the administration of Yasukuni shrine itself has seemed determined to exacerbate matters by not merely maintaining but openly emphasizing its military affiliations. First, it maintains a highly visible war museum on its grounds. There is on display, for instance, a suicide note from a mother who dove off a bridge with her children. How was their death an act of loyalty to the emperor? She jumped so that her husband would not hesitate, out of some lingering sense of family responsibility, to offer himself wholeheartedly as a kamikaze pilot. In the museum there are also numerous suicide notes from kamikaze pilots themselves. One could argue that these displays are merely examples of the heroism, loyalty, and dedication of those who died in the war effort, but not in any way an endorsement of the war itself. This is not the rhetoric, however. Museum exhibits, shrine pamphlets, booklets written for children—all make it clear that such behavior from the war years is an example to all of us. The rhetoric proclaims how wonderful it would be if we all could again have the opportunity to show such loyalty to the emperor and to Japan.

A second way in which the shrine officials goad their critics is the justifications they offer for such practices as the enshrinement of war criminals. One might imagine an argument that Shinto is not about judging good and evil but rather defilement and impurity. Traditionally, as explained in chapter 1, it was never claimed that a *kami*'s actions were necessarily beneficial; many actions have caused calamities for humans. Thus it might be argued that the enshrinement of executed war criminals was part of an act of purification for the defilement in which they had partaken: a way of appeasing restless, violent spirits (such as Michizane's spirit discussed in chapter 3). This is not the conventional line of argument, however. Instead the official Yasukuni website (both the Japanese and English versions) refers to the war crime trials as a "sham" and says that atrocities are a universal characteristic of war for which all warring nations are culpable. Yasukuni leaders have also made public statements about the related "textbook controversy." Asian and Pacific countries have continuously complained that official Japanese schoolbooks always minimize Japan's wartime aggression and play down or omit entirely any mention of such incidents and practices as the "rape of Nanjing" and the enslavement of Korean females as sexual "comfort women" for Japanese troops. The general approach in Yasukuni rebuttals is that since all countries—including the victors—were guilty of such atrocities, to focus on them in textbooks would mislead Japanese students into thinking Japan alone was guilty of such crimes against humanity.

Obviously, then, State Shinto ideology survives on some level in parts of Japanese society. It certainly thrives quite concretely in Yasukuni shrine across the street from the imperial palace in Tokyo. For many Japanese, this ideology is both an embarrassment and a reminder of wartime rhetoric best left forgotten. But Yasukuni shrine goes on. A major part of its ability to survive derives from postwar Japan's inability to sort out the two forms of Shinto spirituality: existential and essentialist. As a result, despite SCAP's efforts during the occupation and despite the continuing efforts of many liberal and radical Japanese, the State Shinto ideology continues to find new forms of institutionalization and public voice. In chapter 6, the final chapter, we will consider some generalizations about why this is the case and look at some options available to Japan for addressing these problems.

The Way Home

This final chapter speculates about Shinto's future and the implications of our study for philosophy, religious studies, and our understanding of spirituality. The chapter has three sections. First we will summarize our findings about Shinto spirituality and outline options for Shinto's further development in light of such problematic phenomena as the Yasukuni shrine controversy. The second section reflects briefly on what our analysis implies for the comparative study of religion, especially what we have learned from our focus on the existential/essentialist dynamic in Shinto spirituality. The third and final section of the chapter explores what our study of Shinto suggests about the nature of spirituality itself. This concern will return us to some issues first raised in chapter 1.

Shinto's Way Home from the Wars

For purposes of review, we can use a chart to compare the major characteristics of existential and essentialist Shinto spiritualities as they now exist in Japan. (See Table 1.) A major problem for Shinto today is that these two forms of spirituality exist alongside each other without much clarity about their precise relation. It is as if there were two separate spiritual traditions known as Shinto. One Shinto has the existential emphasis and is functional, either consciously or unconsciously, in the daily lives of almost all Japanese. The other Shinto is driven by essentialist assumptions and is much more limited in its following. Yet whenever Shinto is conceived as an organized spiritual tradition, its essentialist forms come to the fore because this is the spirituality connected with most major Shinto institutions. After all, who can speak for existential Shinto? No one is in charge; no institution is dedicated to training people in it or teaching them about it; no organization for it exists at all; it does not even have a scripture to study. Any large Japanese bookstore will have a shelf or two of volumes on Shinto for general readers wishing to learn more about their spiritual heritage. Most of these books are written by the experts on Shinto: professors at the major Shinto universities, naturally, or perhaps priests from major Shinto shrines (who were often trained, at least in part, at these universities). As we have seen, these institutions have been the centers for essentialist Shinto scholarship and doctrinal developments linked to the Native Studies movement. The influence of this history is often visible even in the books written today. Ironically, though, the books are generally written by specialists steeped in essentialist Shinto spirituality whereas the general readership for the books often brings a more existential spiritual orientation. If we really think there are two Shintos, this situation would be like being a Buddhist living in a Buddhist country where the only books on Buddhism were written by, say, Christians.

If a Japanese really wants to deepen her or his existential Shinto spirituality, therefore, the place to go may not be the bookstore. The true experts in existential Shinto spirituality are not the scholars and priests who write books but Mom and Pop, Grandma and Grandpa. They carry the heritage of Shinto praxis in its existential form. Of course, in answer to many questions, especially those about the "real meaning" of this ritual behavior or that Shinto term, their answers may often be "I don't know." But this may be the best answer. It tells us three things. First, it is sincere: the true answer is in the mindful heart, not the analytic mind. The elders may not be able to explain it, but perhaps they express it in *how* they think, act, and feel. Sometimes a poet can express or evoke what the philosopher can never quite articulate in rational analysis. The same may be true of the existentially spiritual person. Second, their answer implies that the question asked has not come up in their own experience of "feeling Shinto" and "being Shinto" in an existential way. The question may be legitimate, but this does not mean its answer is crucial to spiritual growth. And third, some kinds of questioning are not just beside the point but actually counterproductive. This was Norinaga's theme in critiquing what he called the "Chinese mentality." If he were alive today, he might have called it the "scientific" or "scholarly" mentality: any approach that

TABLE 1. EXISTENTIAL AND ESSENTIALIST SHINTO COMPARED

Characteristic	Existential Shinto Spirituality	Essentialist Shinto Spirituality
interaction with other religions	syncretism, inclusiveness	distinctiveness, uniqueness, exclusiveness
institutional form	local/regional centers with at most loosely defined national organization	centralized organization coordinated nationally
doctrine	unsystematic collection of key concepts, ideas, values	attempt at systematic, coherent, and comprehensive doctrinal system; development of scriptural canon (*Kojiki* and *Nihonshoki*)
relation to emperor	emperor as chief priest in loosely organized religion	emperor as chief priest and head of state; ritual authority permeates the religious and political context
primary nature of *kami*	wondrous, mysterious presence; sometimes personalized when described in traditional myths and specific practices	personal deities, especially those of creation; by extension related to all creation as by-product of these deities; can be protective force for nation
primary nature of *tama*	spiritual, vital energy or power related to *kami* presence in all things; can be specified as individual soul, collective force, or more generally energy (or life-force) not separate from matter	metaphysical, supernatural life-energy or power immanent in this *kami*-created world mainly in concentrated source points (imperial *tama;* a family's ancestral *tama;* the collective *tama* of the dead at Yasukuni); these source points may infuse individual's soul (*mitama* or *tamashii)*
focus of praxis	practices not correlated with a metaphysical or even fully articulated doctrinal system; practices considered "traditional" and serve people's everyday sense of connectedness and belonging; praxis inclusive, somewhat fluid	justification for praxis (metapraxis) strongly developed and typically linked with an articulated metaphysical system; layer of doctrinal meaning tends to be an overlay on religious experience such that orthopraxy, orthodoxy, heterodoxy, and heteropraxy can be key issues

thinks "I don't know" can only be the beginning, not the appropriate end, of an investigation. The scientist's "I don't know" triggers a research grant proposal. For the professor to say "I don't know" is a confession, not a profession. This mentality, as Norinaga argued, cannot accept the wondrous, the marvelous, and the awesome for being just what they are. Because this mentality cannot accept such phenomena at face value, it never really comes face-to-face with the wondrous awe. Such experiences get peripheralized, filed away as something odd to talk about at the tavern on a cold winter night with friends, but not to be taken seriously in one's "real life."

Having such existential Shinto sensibilities, many Japanese today are wary of politicians and Shinto leaders who display a normative, prescriptive, or essentialist bias. Their essentialist Shinto spirituality is often so thoroughly interwoven with a nationalist, right-wing political agenda that many Japanese hold them in disdain for "trying to refight the war." They hope that as the decades pass, the old essentialist Shinto of the foreign war years will die out as the people of that generation pass away. As the Yasukuni controversy indicates, however, this does not seem to be happening. The problem is that the essentialist and existential Shinto spiritualities are not completely separate. In fact, they are in an internal relationship with a great deal of overlap. And today the essentialists control the nature of that overlap. Again, a personal anecdote illustrates the predicament.

A couple of years ago I was staying in a Tokyo hotel near Yasukuni shrine. I like the area because it is a short distance from the bookstore district and, with the extensive grounds of the imperial palace and Yasukuni shrine nearby, it has pockets of quiet in the otherwise noisy city. One day I awoke early and decided to take a stroll before breakfast. I meandered over to Yasukuni shrine and sauntered through the grounds. It was a clear summer Sunday morning and at six o'clock the area was quiet and peaceful, not yet crowded, hot, or humid. Even the famous Yasukuni doves were just beginning to move about. A few perched on the huge *torii* arching over the main walkway to the shrine building, appropriate since *"torii"* literally means "bird perch." The overall effect was that I could "feel Shinto" as described in chapter 1. Like the businessman from that chapter, I went up to the outer gate of the shrine and followed standard protocol for purification, offering,

and bowing. On that quiet, early Sunday morning, I felt the connectedness associated with Shinto. After my ritualized visit, I turned to go
back down the walkway leading out of the shrine. After I had taken
several steps, two elderly men startled me by popping out of the
wooded area alongside the path. By their dress and rakes, I realized
they were groundskeepers. Solemnly they bowed and then in polite
Japanese thanked me for my visit and the respect I had shown. I
smiled, bowed back politely, and went my way quietly. I had not seen
them before, even when just a minute or two earlier, a Japanese man
had done exactly what I had done. Obviously they would have seen
him, too, but they had not stopped him. Their special expression of
gratitude was likely related to my being a foreigner, presumably an
American.

While eating breakfast, I reflected on this encounter and began to
feel uneasy. I wished I could have gone back and spoken to the two
groundskeepers, but because more than an hour had passed, the
moment was gone. I scrutinized my discomfort. At Yasukuni, I had
just had one of those "feeling Shinto" experiences that were for me so
closely tied to inclusive, existential sensitivities. Yet what were those
two men thinking? Since they seemed to be in their mid-sixties, I
quickly calculated that although they might not have been old enough
to serve in the war, they probably had at least some memories of it and
perhaps even had older siblings who had served. Might they even have
relatives enshrined in Yasukuni? If that were true and they were showing gratitude for my respecting their deceased family members, I was
pleased they appreciated my actions. Yet this was summer, the season
of the annual Yasukuni shrine controversy. The media were just beginning to stir the embers. Were the elderly men relating my own visit to
these events? Did they see my behavior as a sign that I agree with the
Yasukuni and government officials rather than with the protesting
Chinese, Koreans, and liberal Japanese? If so, I wished I had talked
with them to explain my position. But what would I have said? Perhaps: "Maybe you don't understand: I was just using this place as a
holographic entry point to access the wondrous presence of reality as
a whole. Please don't assume my actions were in any way a political
statement related to the Yasukuni controversy. My Shinto-related
behavior was strictly existential, not essentialist." If I had said that,

they would not have had the slightest idea of what I was talking about. The very distinction between essentialist and existential spirituality is not in the Japanese vocabulary for talking about Shinto. The problem is that even if I think of my spiritual experience as existential, my actions lend themselves to being interpreted by others as an endorsement of essentialist spirituality. Undoubtedly today's right-wing political conservatives count every Japanese visit to a Shinto shrine (which statistically is on the increase) as an endorsement of their own political agenda.

This episode illustrates, I think, that the two Shinto spiritualities are not separate religious traditions but instead overlap in an internal relation with each other. This observation leads to further complications. First of all, there are serious terminological problems in trying to divorce them. State Shinto's essentialist ideology, indoctrinated daily into the Japanese people for the first half of the twentieth century, has profoundly influenced today's understanding of Shinto vocabulary—not only spiritual but also psychological, metaphysical, metapractical, and political. If I tried to describe in Japanese my own spiritual experience at Yasukuni, I would inevitably use traditional terms like "*tama*," "*kami*," "*makoto no kokoro*," and "*mitama*." Yet in the past two centuries every one of these key terms has been glossed by essentialist Shinto interpretations. In Table 1, for example, we find many of the same terms in both columns, but the meanings are sometimes quite different. Because of the nuances accrued through many decades of essentialist analysis, the ancient Shinto terms are no longer ingenuous. In this book, written in English for a Western audience, these Japanese terms were no doubt new to most readers. Therefore I have been able to control the way they were presented—alerting us to nuances that drive the discourse about them in different directions. To discuss Shinto in its own terms in Japanese, however, often implicates essentialist assumptions invisibly into the discourse.

A prominent contemporary Japanese philosopher, Ueda Shizuteru, aptly calls this sort of phenomenon a philosophical "tug of war over words." In reflecting on the problems Kyoto school philosophers faced in the militarist 1930s and 1940s, he has noted that certain philosophers used terms like "*kokutai*" in their writings. As we have seen, "*kokutai*" was a favorite term of the Japanese imperialists. Yet in so doing, he claims, these philosophers were often not endorsing government policies but in fact trying to undermine them by giving the key terms of their ideology a less nationalistic and militarist spin. In that era, no one could publicly deny the reality of *kokutai* (at least without facing the likely consequence of imprisonment or worse), but perhaps the venomous words could be defanged. Such contestations over the meaning of central political terms is not limited to Japan, of course. Consider the term "family values" in American politics. Every U.S. politician is in favor of them; it is political suicide to be against family values. So the battle shifts to what the term *really* means. Can single-parent families have family values? Can gay or lesbian couples have them? Can atheists have them? Can working parents have them? The tug of war over words is under way.

Shinto faces a similar problem today, but the situation is worse. There is a fixed domain of terms used to express Shinto spirituality, regardless of whether that spirituality is existential or essentialist. The only issue is what the terms actually mean. Contemporary scholarly interpretations ultimately trace back to the Native Studies movement and what had come to be a distinctively essentialist agenda. To reclaim the meaning of these terms in accord with the existential column in Table 1, the most obvious strategy would be to go back to the significance of the terms before the Native Studies movement colored their meaning with its own ideological agenda. But this policy runs into a further obstacle. The Native Studies movement holds the patent on the very enterprise of "returning to the ancient way." The impact of Native Studies scholars in the field of historical philology is overwhelming. They did all the groundwork for mapping the field. To try to find the way back home to the "original" meaning of terms, one finds oneself using a Native Studies map with its limited-access highways. Skilled scholars can, of course, painstakingly try to dismantle some of the nuances essentialism has read into the terms, but the project is daunting and so technical that it would not have much public impact, at least for a very long time.

There is one further disadvantage that existential Shinto spirituality would face in its tug of war over words with essentialist Shinto spirituality. This one is more a philosophical difficulty: on what grounds can one argue that Shinto should not be prescriptive? To say that Shinto should not be prescriptive is itself to prescribe what Shinto should be. To criticize essentialist spirituality, an existential spirituality has to fight the battle on essentialist spirituality's own intellectual turf. Existential spirituality has to cloak itself in an essentialist discourse of its own. As we will see later in this chapter, this general paradox has significance not only for Shinto but also for the history of religions in general. For Shinto, the tug of war over words amounts to arguing that the existential column in Table 1 is "genuine" Shinto and the essentialist column represents a politically motivated "distortion," or at least "restriction," of true Shinto.

To see how this would work out in practice, let us imagine a new form of essentialist Shinto discourse that might arise as a criticism against the old State Shinto essentialist ideology. For brevity's sake, we will call this a "neo-essentialist" form of Shinto spirituality and its philosophical target "paleo-essentialist" Shinto spirituality. Consider, for example, how such a neo-essentialist Shinto could treat the meaning of "*kami.*" Freeing itself from the standard account of Shinto discussed in chapter 3, it could argue that the *essential* meaning of "*kami*" is simply "wondrously awe-inspiring presence." This would make the defining characteristic of "Shinto" (the way of *kami*) a belief in, and praxis responsive to, any such presence. If a particular neo-essentialist Shinto finds the emperor to have such presence, the believer would consider the emperor *kami.* Yet if another does not, this itself does not necessarily make the person "not Shinto." Here we find the difference from the paleo-essentialist ideology. According to the neo-essentialist position, so long as one believes *something* is *kami,* this suffices to qualify the person as "Shinto." The emperor may or may not be on the list of what a believer considers to be holographic entry points for one's own Shinto spirituality. Similarly, a neo-essentialist Shinto might allow Shinto followers to think of the celestial *kami* of creation as either actually existent persons or as metaphors. So long as someone considers creation itself wondrous and awe-inspiring, this would be enough to identify the person as "Shinto."

At first glance, neo-essentialist Shinto might seem no more than the old existential Shinto. But in fact it is not. Neo-essentialist Shinto is *prescriptive,* not descriptive, insofar as it argues that if one is Shinto, one must believe in a world full of wondrous, awe-inspiring presence and should engage that presence experientially. The essentialism maintained by the neo-essentialist Shinto envisioned here may be as minimal as possible in order to include a Shinto pluralism that allows different people to find the holographic entry point to this presence in different ways and at different sites. (This is one way it resembles the openness of the old existential Shinto spirituality.) Yet neo-essentialist Shinto can still prescribe that to be Shinto one must find that awe-inspiring presence *somewhere*. This practically boils down to saying that what we have in this book called "feeling Shinto" is essential to Shinto identity. Neo-essentialist Shinto may require more than this for its core, but it can still be quite pluralistic in the kinds of things that might serve as holographic entry points for such feelings. From this neo-essentialist position, it can criticize State Shinto essentialism for being wrong-headed—not because it is not Shinto but because it mistakenly says there is only one kind of essentialist Shinto with a very limited understanding of what can qualify as *kami* or *tama* or a holographic entry point. In developing its critique of paleo-essentialist Shinto, it can make historical arguments against the Native Studies version of what qualifies as "pure" Shinto. For example, it might question why Buddhist-Shinto syncretism is a defilement rather than an enhancement of Shinto (giving it new holographic entry points and new terminology for talking about the experience at the heart of Shinto spirituality). After all, the neo-essentialist might argue, was not the ancient Emperor Shōmu by definition *kami,* and did he not spiritually embrace Buddhism as well as Shinto?

This line of thought opens the door to the possibility of a range of neo-essentialist Shinto groups falling between the narrowly defined, tightly organized paleo-essentialism of Shrine Shinto and the much more open neo-essentialist form just outlined. There can be a plurality of essentialist Shinto groups. One could argue, in fact, that such is already the case. There are, for example, both the descendants of the original Sect Shinto groups as well as various *kami*-related "new religions" that have arisen since then. Many draw just as directly on existential sensitivities but have nonetheless developed systems of doctrine and praxis that give them an essentialist core identity. In these doctrinal formulations, many avoid the ultranationalism and ethnocentrism of State Shinto ideology and find their own preferred holographic entry points. For many of the Shinto-related new religions, for example, the founder of the sect serves such a role. Such a pluralism of neo-essentialist forms of Shinto spirituality entails that no single form can speak as if theirs is the only kind of Shinto—any more than, say, the Pope or the Dalai Lama can speak for all Christians or all Buddhists. Let us now apply this pluralistic understanding of essentialist Shinto to the Yasukuni controversy.

The political entanglements in the Yasukuni controversy are partly unraveled if one insists that Yasukuni represents only one of many Shinto sects. Specifically, since State Shinto ideas cannot be outlawed in a society guaranteeing freedom of expression, all the law can ensure is that wherever State Shinto ideology is institutionalized, it is always by definition deemed a *religious* institution. Furthermore, the law can ensure that not one yen of public money flows into the coffers of such an institution. Nor can the government legally claim a right to enshrine people at Yasukuni over the wishes of, say, the family of the deceased. The claim to this right rests in a particular *religious* metaphysical doctrine about the nature of *tama* and the protection of Japan. Following the interpretations developed in this book, there is no such entity as a "nonsectarian" and "nonreligious" Shinto institution or organization. By definition, every Shinto institution is a sectarian institution and cannot speak with any authority for all Japanese—indeed not even for all Shinto Japanese. Let us also stop mincing words about whether Shrine Shinto was a "religion." Of course it was. Indeed it was not only a religion but, its protests notwithstanding, it was a "*shūkyō*" as well. Recall that the Japanese were hesitant to call their spiritual traditions "*shūkyō*" because the word had associations with dogmatic teachings, exclusivism, strict prescriptive practices, and metaphysical essentialism. If there were ever a Japanese religious institution that had these characteristics, it was Shrine Shinto. Given this understanding, one can argue that the government activities at Yasukuni have been legally problematic since the Meiji Constitution of 1889, not just since the postwar constitution of 1947. This leaves some questions about the buildings across the street from Yasukuni: the imperial palace complex. The future of Shinto cannot be discussed without including the future of the imperial system.

The quandary about the imperial system derives from the

emperor's being both the chief priest of Shinto and the titular head of state. The latter designation is not problematic so long as "titular" means the emperor is the head of state in name only—that is, if imperial rule is in every sense strictly symbolic and not derived from a sacred basis. This thinking accords with the imperial proclamation of 1946 stating that the throne is "not based in mere legends and myths" and the "emperor is not divine." Politically speaking, then, the emperor is not *kami*. This interpretation follows from the Japanese constitution: the succession of the throne is determined by birth, but if there is a throne at all it is by the democratic consent of the Japanese people. In this legal respect, the Japanese emperor (or empress) plays a role not much different from European kings or queens in other modern-day democratic states with monarchies.

This secularized political role of the throne has ramifications for the emperor's being a holographic entry point for Japanese identity. Following the line of argument just developed, this function can continue if, but only if, it is based on secular rather than religious grounds. That is: the emperor can serve a function of "reflecting the whole" in the way a national flag or national anthem (or, it might be argued, the monarch of the United Kingdom) might. Given the history of State Shinto ideology, however, this has to be carefully monitored. From a legal and political standpoint, treating the emperor as such an entry point must be both strictly secular and strictly voluntary for Japanese citizens. One should not be arrested for being disloyal or disrespectful to the emperor any more than an American can be arrested for burning a flag in political protest of U.S. policy. Put in historical terminology, the government cannot require a Japanese citizen to "revere the emperor," though I suppose it could still, at least constitutionally, tell people to "expel the barbarians." Moreover, the constitution ties the emperor's holographic function to the consent of the people. Just as citizens can choose to change their flag or national anthem, the holographic function of the emperor is open to democratic reinterpretation through the years. There can be nothing eternal about the role of the emperor as nominal head of state.

The other aspect of the emperor's role—the emperor as the chief priest of Shinto—is more problematic. As we have argued, to construe Shinto (any kind of Shinto) as "nonreligious" was an act of sophistry perpetrated by State Shinto ideologues. To claim, therefore, that the emperor is the "chief priest of Shinto" is clearly a religious claim. Indeed it derives from a certain metaphysical understanding of the *kami* nature of the imperial family. Since this is a religious belief, individual Japanese are constitutionally guaranteed the right to either accept or reject it. Furthermore, by the neo-essentialist Shinto suggested here, the belief that the emperor is *kami* may not even be required of people who can be legitimately identified as "Shinto." Of course, many groups of Shinto followers do accept the *kami* nature of the emperor. And for them the emperor is the chief priest of their religion. Viewed in this light, the conclusion is that the emperor is the titular head of state for all Japanese people but the chief priest for only *some,* but not all, Shinto Japanese. Any sacerdotal functions (as contrasted with functions related to being titular head of state) should be supported through the donations of these religious adherents, not by the state. In practice, it may be very difficult to sort out all the political from the religious functions of the emperor, but the importance of the principle should be appreciated.

We have been assuming, of course, that the emperor will have a continuing role in Japanese politics and, at least for some people, in Shinto praxis as well. But there are other options. One option is that the imperial system could be entirely dissolved. Given the current popular Japanese fondness for the institution, this seems unlikely, at least in the near future. A second possibility would be to divest the emperor of all political functions, making him something analogous to the Pope in Roman Catholicism. Then all financial support for the institution would come from the people who feel religiously connected to it and none at all from the state. The third option is to divest the emperor of all religious, Shinto-related functions. In this case, the role would be more like that of current European monarchs. The state could then support the imperial institution, but the emperor would be banned from any sacerdotal activities.

Such alternatives are, of course, for the Japanese themselves to consider. The purpose of this discussion is not to create a new form of Shinto or tell the Japanese how to understand their imperial institutions. The point is only to show that a neo-essentialist Shinto could evolve in ways that do not reinforce State Shinto ideology but do preserve the importance of Shinto in Japanese culture. Indeed, if such a neo-essentialist Shinto spirituality were to predominate, existential Shinto spirituality could still thrive. As we have seen, the nineteenth century brought the demise of Shinto-Buddhist syncretism and existential Shinto spirituality lost much of its former philosophical justification. State Shinto ideology filled this void. A neo-essentialist Shinto might offer the sensitivities of existential Shinto spirituality a new rationale, one that is neither disguised Buddhism nor disguised State Shinto nationalism.

Homing in on Spirituality in Religious Studies

Let us now leave the specificities of the Japanese Shinto context and consider how the existential/essentialist distinction might assist in the study of religions in general. The distinction can be applied to many, if not most, religions insofar as it delineates two ways spiritual experience may interface with doctrines and praxis. Over the past few decades, there has been a pendular swing within religious studies in how to treat "religious experience." A half century ago, the nature of this experience (often presumed to be universal across many, if not all, traditions) was central to answering the question "what is religion?" Religion scholars emphasized terms like "ultimate concern" (Paul Tillich) or "hierophany" (Mircea Eliade) or "experience of the numinous" (Rudolf Otto). In short: the assumption was often that one could not understand religion without understanding its personal, experiential ground. Too often this meant ignoring or marginalizing the social, political, and economic structures of religious institutions. For the past two or three decades, however, the pendulum has swung in the opposite direction. Indeed it has swung so much that many scholars consider the experiential to be no more than the side effect or epiphenomenon of social conditions for control and authority. Ideology is primary; experience is derivative, they claim. By this assessment, personal experience may come down to no more than a neo-Marxist "false consciousness" or a neo-Freudian "libidinal drive."

In this book, the existential/essentialist analysis has allowed us to explore both the experiential and institutional poles. We found, on the one hand, that we could not give a full picture of Shinto as a religion without including some description of personal spiritual experience. This was a major concern of chapters 1 and 2. On the other hand, chapters 3, 4, and 5 outlined the institutional, social, and political developments that have contextualized these experiences through Japanese history. This book has shown how at times the social and political institutions were loosely structured and inclusivist and, at other times, tightly organized and exclusivist. Chapters 3 to 5 outlined three phases of Shinto's historical development: (1) from the primordial, preliterate, or prehistoric existential stage up through the political, social, textual, and artistic processes of the seventh and eighth centuries that sowed the seeds of essentialist Shinto; (2) the dormancy of essentialist Shinto development throughout most of the millennium of Shinto-Buddhist syncretism; and (3) the emergence of Native Studies in the late Tokugawa period leading to the predominance of essentialist Shinto in the modern period and leaving in its wake the still-to-be-resolved dynamics of postwar Shinto. To generalize further the dynamic between essentialist and existential spirituality, a few points merit further attention here.

First we note that, although stage 2 seems to lack much essentialist Shinto development, this era was not devoid of essentialist religious forms. That is: Buddhist-Shinto syncretism contained many elements of essentialist *Buddhist* spirituality. Buddhist metaphysics and metapraxis prescribed to some extent what was orthodoxy and orthopraxis for the Shinto side of the syncretism—and this essentialist Buddhist assimilation of Shinto became one of the key targets for essentialist Shinto spirituality developed in stage 3. In other words: during phase 2, essentialist Buddhism overwhelmed the essentialist Shinto tendencies developing in the eighth century; during phase 3, essentialist Shinto was reestablished in such a way as to eradicate essentialist Buddhist influences. Viewed in these terms, although the Japanese dynamic was almost completely intranational, the situation may relate in interesting ways to the study of postcolonial religious phenomena in other parts of the world.

Let us consider, for example, some postcolonial developments related to Christianity. With European and U.S. imperialism, many colonized peoples became at least partially Christianized, either vol-

untarily or through some degree of coercion. With subsequent independence, the postcolonial peoples have had the freedom to rethink
the relation between Christianity and the indigenous religious ideas,
values, and practices preceding colonization. There have been various
responses to this opportunity, two of which we will discuss here: resuscitating the precolonial tradition or modifying the colonial religion to
include precolonial elements. In the first case, the emphasis has sometimes been on the revival of ancient religious forms preexisting the
introduction of Christianity—in effect going back to the indigenous
rather than foreign-influenced spirituality. For example, there has
been a revitalization of various shamanistic or animistic practices and
ideas among native groups in the Americas, Asia, the Pacific, and
Africa. This process parallels in some ways the Native Studies movement in Japan with its attempt to eliminate Buddhist (or Confucian)
elements in Shinto. Yet as we saw in the Japanese case, recovering
what was "lost" often involves some systematic reflection and doctrinal development. That is: in the attempt to recapture the past, there is
often an accompanying attempt to justify the ideas and practices of
the past. As a result, the indigenous religion starts assuming essentialist modalities characteristic of the colonial religion: systematizing doctrine, developing metapractical justifications drawing on some previously inchoate metaphysics, and so forth. Once a foreign essentialist
form of religiosity has taken hold in a culture, the most viable way of
recapturing the "traditional" and "native" is to exclude the foreign elements. This process requires (at least to some extent) an essentializing
of the precolonial tradition in order to justify what to exclude (the
colonial influences). In effect, this casts the traditional into a more
essentialist form—even if that form was not originally part of the
tradition before colonization. The result is a well-known paradox: to
recapture the past for preservation, one has to alter it.

Foreign scholars of religion, often from the former colonizing
countries, may inadvertently play a role in this alteration. As we have
seen in chapter 3's discussion of the "standard narrative" for describing Shinto, essentialist Shinto fit the categories with which Western
(mainly Christian and Jewish) scholars were familiar (sacred texts,
central authority, religion/politics interface, systematic doctrinal sys-

tem, cosmogonic narrative, and the like). To a great extent, therefore, these foreign scholars fell into describing Shinto in the essentialist terms favored by State Shinto ideology—thereby reinforcing the ideology itself by granting it international currency. A similar distortion has occurred in Western scholarship's clumping all precolonial religions into something called "primal," "primordial," "archaic," or "indigenous" religions. By grouping a variety of religions from around the world into a single category, Western scholars have struggled to find a common characteristic among them—thereby essentializing them all in one fell swoop (and making them collectively resemble more closely essentialist religious modes).

Native American religions present an interesting case of this sort. The United States guarantees Native Americans the legal right to practice their religion. Yet to make a legal case that certain U.S. policies are violating this right, Native American groups must articulate exactly what in their religion is being violated. This requires a systematic characterization of the particular Native American group's religious doctrines and practices: exactly what essential qualities make it a "traditional Native American religion" and therefore deserving of special government protection? The legal force of the complaint is diminished, for example, if there is any sign that the Native American practice or belief borrowed on nonnative traditions (the premise is that syncretism cannot be traditional) or if the practice or belief is somehow fluid rather than fixed (the premise is that tradition is unchanging). As a result, even though the Native American religion might have once had an existential form, to prove itself "traditional" it must present itself in an essentialist modality. To preserve their very existence, Native American religions have to assume the garb of essentialist spirituality alongside the essentialist spirituality of Christianity, Judaism, or Islam. The parallel with our discussion of the agenda for a neo-essentialist Shinto spirituality is striking.

Besides resuscitating and reformulating precolonial tradition by giving it an essentialist form, there is another common postcolonial response to preserving aspects of precolonial spirituality. This is to modify the colonial religion to include these precolonial elements. Today this is a vital source of innovative Christian theologies and liturgies, for example. Pentecostal and charismatic forms of Christianity are successful in many postcolonial settings because they so often resonate with precolonial religious ideas, values, and practices. Ritual aspects of shamanism and indigenous spirit possession rites may therefore be integrated into Christian Pentecostal and charismatic practices. On the theological rather than liturgical side, some Chinese theologians, for instance, have interpreted the relation between God the Father and humans as one of filial piety (a Confucian idea foreign to Abrahamic conceptions of God). What we find in such cases is that the colonial religion (in these examples Christianity) is revitalized in a postcolonial context by drawing on religions preexisting Christianity in that region of the world. This is analogous in some ways with esoteric Buddhism's ability to establish itself in Japan by resonating with pre-Buddhist Shinto values, ideas, and practices. A similar phenomenon occurred in Tibetan Buddhism's interactions with pre-Buddhist forms of Tibetan religion.

To sum up: reflections on the existential/essentialist dynamic can influence religious studies in several ways. First, they can reveal patterns in the historical development of religious traditions. (Was Constantine's involvement the point at which Christianity moved from a predominantly existential to essentialist religion?) Second, the dynamic may shed light on the different contexts for the meaning and use of key religious terms. (Can we differentiate existential and essentialist understandings of terms like "jihad" or "Zionism" as we differentiated existential and essentialist understandings of terms like "*kami*" or "*tama*"?) Third, in studying various religions, scholars might question whether their scholarly approach leads them to look primarily for essentialist rather than existential aspects of religious phenomena. (How can one balance the experiential and social/political/economic aspects of religious phenomena?) And fourth, the existential/essentialist dynamic can itself be a focus in religious studies. (Are there any cases, for example, of a culture in which essentialist religion became dominant and then was succeeded by existential? Or is the transition always from existential to essentialist?) This question leads us into the final section of this chapter: what this study of Shinto might reveal about the nature of spirituality itself.

Shinto Spirituality as a Way Home

In these final pages, let us move the discussion from scholarly analysis to a more personal religious or philosophical reflection. As a scholar, I have tried in this book to say something fair about Shinto spirituality, giving it a balanced and, to the extent possible, objective hearing. Now as a philosopher of religion, indeed as a human being, I want to go further. Chapter 1 claimed that the experience of "feeling Shinto" need not be limited to Japanese. Does this mean there is something about Shinto spirituality that speaks to the human situation at large? In Shinto, existential religious dimensions predominated for a very long time, continuing even into modern times. Perhaps for this reason the encounter with Shinto can sharpen our focus on aspects of spirituality that may be found in many religious traditions but, because of their particular cultural and historical development, not so obviously. At least in my own encounter with Shinto spirituality over the years, I have gained from it a deeper understanding of spirituality itself. I can cite four areas: the importance of connectedness to feeling whole; the appreciation of awe; the function of ritual praxis; and the lingering nostalgia for a bygone existential spirituality.

First, it is hardly surprising to point out that spirituality has something to do with feeling connected. In many religions, this connectedness has a strongly transcendent dimension. That is: because of a connection to something behind, beyond, or at the base of the ordinary world, the spiritual person's relation to this world—its people, its natural phenomena, its social fabric—may be transformed. There is a fad in some circles to say that such religions are, therefore, "transcendent" rather than "immanent" in form. For the most part, when we get down to concrete examples, the bifurcation is not so absolute and such labels may be misleading. Even in, for instance, a monotheistic religion wherein there is a belief in a transcendent God who created and continues in some way to sustain the world, close examination often shows that the actual spirituality is experienced immanently as well as transcendently. In other words: the experiential connection with every person and every thing derives from a conviction that all are based on a common source. Hence: "God is everywhere," "we are all brothers and sisters" (for St. Francis of Assisi this explicitly included animals and natural objects), and even "all is one." In this regard, God may be metaphysically transcendent to the world but experientially known primarily in and through the world. For this reason, it may not be all that useful to try to classify religions as transcendent or immanent. Perhaps a better point of focus might be to ask whether the connectedness to the sacred is an external or internal relation.

For many monotheistic religions, the immanent connectedness among things is understood via an *external* relation to God. The sacred is the *"R"* that connects *A* to *B* in Figure 1 from chapter 1. For Shinto, by contrast, the immanent connectedness is inherent; the connection is part of what *A* and *B* are *in themselves* (Figure 2). In some respects, essentialist Shinto moved away from this understanding with its emphasis on *kami* as creating deities and its concern for the somewhat individualized *mitama.* Yet by maintaining the holographic model between part and whole, even the State Shinto ideology ultimately avoided, for the most part, an analysis based simply on external relations.

This discussion suggests that spirituality may be understood as an emphasis on connectedness—on feeling at home in the world. Differences in spirituality might then be understood as, at least in some part, related to how "connectedness" is conceived and experienced. Most, maybe all, religions are immanent insofar as they impact upon the everyday through second-nature ideas, values, and behavior, as well as the ritualized commemoration of life's major events. Because of this immanence, the world is lived as spiritually infused. Yet the form of immanence, how it is interpreted, taught, and experienced, may differ from case to case. For especially the last four or five hundred years, for example, Christianity has in its mainstream doctrinal development generally excluded panentheism, the idea that God is literally in every thing that exists (and yet is more than just that). In doing so, it has marginalized or excluded from its own spirituality some experiences of the kind central to Shinto. Perhaps something could be recaptured here. The holographic analysis we used to explain Shinto spirituality so fruitfully might be of help in this enterprise.

The second area to explore is the importance of awe in spirituality. Again it is hardly innovative to claim religion has something to do with wonder, mystery, and awe. Yet Shinto, as a contemporary religion in a highly technological society, is striking in its insistence that awe is not to be understood or comprehended in any systematic way. As noted in chapter 1, the point of Shinto practice is often more to make one feel at home with awe rather than try to understand or control it. In many respects, as the paleo-essentialist Shinto spirituality evolved over the past two centuries, some of this tendency has been undermined. In fact, even in the period of Buddhist-Shinto syncretism it could be argued that esoteric Buddhist doctrine was used to explain the source of awe and bring it under intellectual and spiritual control. In effect, existential Shinto spirituality could thrive under Buddhist-Shinto syncretism because essentialist Buddhist spirituality took care of all the philosophical explaining and justifying.

In our own modern world, one result of the predominance of scientific thinking is that today our initial response to the awesome is to try to understand it rather than to stand under it. Instead of filling us with a sense of humility before the unknown, awe has come to challenge us as only the not-yet-known. "I don't know" has become an ego-bruising admission of ignorance instead of—as it was for Socrates—a sign of wisdom. When Malunkyaputta asked the Buddha whether time has a beginning, the Buddha was silent. So too was Jesus when Pilate asked him, "What is truth?" As we experience the starry heavens above us, our scientific impulse is to behold an enigma to be analyzed. Hubbell telescopes, space exploration, mathematical modeling—all come to our aid. That is fine. But let us never allow the impulse to understand the firmament outshine the awe and wonder of simply standing under it, feeling ourselves to be inherently part of it and it part of ourselves.

The third lesson about spirituality suggested by our encounter with Shinto is the importance of ritual in sensitizing people to the connectedness we have just discussed. The businessman in chapter 1 was quite puzzled when asked about the "meaning" or "purpose" of his ritualistic visit to the shrine on the way to work. Our discussion of such Shinto behavior illustrates three points about the relation of ritual to spirituality. In the first place, ritual's function may not be conscious, and making its meaning clear may not even deepen its spirituality. As we saw in the analogy of visiting a friend, to articulate a purpose is to make the visit merely a means instead of an end in itself. Friends often say, "Don't be a stranger. You don't need a reason to drop by." Some ritualistic forms merely affirm connectedness without ulterior motive. If I am, to whatever extent, formed by my internal relations with others, then when I am with those others I am more fully myself. Another way ritual sheds light on spirituality is in its repetition. In a consumer culture stressing entertainment, the priority is on innovation. Marketing demands that we not be satisfied redoing what we have already done with what we already have. We saw in chapter 2 that Shinto emphasizes "freshness," not "newness." This suggests renewal rather than innovation or simple repetition. Ritual is perhaps most effective when the old patterns are practiced anew. Ritual connects the present with the past, the *kokoro* with the body, the individual with the community. And, finally, the mention of the body is a reminder of the somatic dimension to repeated action. The more we need to learn something through repetition, the more conscious we become of the body. In this regard, the connection between spirituality and ritual intensifies our awareness that spirituality is not separate from corporeality. Words related to spirituality, such as *pneuma* in Greek, *prāṇa* in Sanskrit, *qi* in Chinese, *ruaḥ* in Hebrew, are not contrasted with the somatic. In fact, many such terms are either directly or indirectly associated with "breath." Ritual breathes life into the spiritual. Ritual is re-spiration.

And fourth, let us consider the nostalgia for existential religious forms. In our postmodern contexts, we are often rightly suspicious of nostalgia as a romanticized construction of a past that never was. Nostalgia often serves ideologies of power by allowing them to disguise change as a return to normalcy: the rhetoric is that power is not being used to coerce change, but rather to undo factors that have corrupted an original purity. As the past takes on the tint of cultural or spiritual authority, the institutions of political authority, to sustain their power, will try to control the intellectual reconstruction of that past. Once a former era is valorized as a time of virginal purity, abusive ideologues will violate it to enhance their own sense of power or pleasure. Nothing shows this better than the transformation of Native Studies from a spiritual-aesthetic project into a political ideology of the state. Shinto presents an excellent case study of the dangers in nostalgia.

Altar at Futami
The altar frames the Wedded Rocks of Futami and includes
a frog (kaeru) *reminding visitors about the importance of*
returning home (kaeru).

But is there not something positive to be said for nostalgia, especially when it is expressed as a desire to resuscitate existential forms of spirituality? Nostalgia can keep tradition alive so that it can be renewed in ritual. Nostalgia can instill a sense of awe for the accomplishments of the past, setting the basis for a hopeful engagement in the future. A nostalgia for animism, community, and ritual performance seems to be driving a renewed sense of spiritual participation in both mainstream and new religions around the world. Even ecological awareness may arise from a nostalgia for a way of living in which humanity used to be a responsive part of nature rather than its manager or exploiter. Etymologically, "ecology" means the "study of home." Ecology is not about managing or controlling the world, but about feeling at home in it. Shinto nostalgia harks back to such values.

In conclusion, then, because of the distinctive tensions between its existential and essentialist forms, Shinto presents us with the two faces of nostalgia. There is the kind of nostalgia nurtured to lend authority to state control. And there is the kind of nostalgia that beckons us back to a form of connectedness that has been all but erased by the rise of scientific thinking, dependence on technology, and consumerism. Since etymologies have played a central role throughout this study, let us conclude with one more. The etymology of the word "nostalgia" is the "ache" (-algia) to "return home" (nostos). And this ache to return home is the aspect of spirituality that Shinto so well exemplifies. We all probably remember feeling it at some point. If we should forget, the frogs of Futami will remind us.

Appendix
Pronouncing Japanese Names and Terms

An English speaker can effectively use the Hepburn romanization of Japanese to achieve a rough approximation of correct pronunciation. The paragraphs preceded by an asterisk are probably the most essential; violation of these rules will often make one's pronunciation of a word unintelligible to a native speaker.

Syllables. A Japanese syllable contains one and only one vowel sound. Thus a syllable may be a single letter (a vowel) or a grouping of a vowel preceded by one or two consonants. All syllables end with a vowel sound, never a consonant. Each syllable has equal stress. Hence flower arranging in Japanese, *"ikebana,"* is pronounced more like "eek-kay-bah-nah" than "eek-kay-BAH-nah."

**Vowels.* There are five vowel sounds, all familiar to English speakers. Pronounce "o, e, i, a" as in the notes of the musical scale "do, re, mi, fa." Pronounce "u" as in the English "put." Thus *"sake"* (Japanese rice wine) is pronounced "sah-kay" not "sah-kee." A vowel may also be nasalized and elongated to two syllables in length. This is indicated by adding "n'" to the end of the syllable. At the end of the word, the apostrophe is dropped. (This is not to be confused with the regular consonant sound "n," which occurs always before a vowel or the consonant "y.")

**Long Vowels.* The vowels "o" and "u" (and less frequently "a, e, i") also occur as long vowels two syllables in length and designated with a macron, such as "ō" and "ū." In this case the vowel sound is simply extended to twice its usual length. For example, "ō" is like saying in English "hell<u>o o</u>ver there" where the two "o" sounds merge into a single "o" double in length. This book follows common English usage in dropping the macron from these eight well-known Japanese words: Shintō, shōgun, Tōkyō, Kyōto, sumō, Honshū, Kyūshū, Ōsaka.

Diphthongs. There are no diphthongs in Japanese (combinations of vowels like "ou" pronounced together in one syllable as in the English "ought" or "pout"). Instead, each occurrence of a vowel is a new syllable. Thus *"geisha"* is pronounced "gay-ee-sha" not "gee-sha."

Consonants. Most consonants are pronounced about as in English (although generally a little more forward in the mouth). Only a few need special comment:

*"g" is always hard like the first, not the second, "g" in the English word "garage." For the latter, the Hepburn romanization uses "j."

*"y" is always a consonant followed by a vowel sound as in the English "yo-yo." It is never a vowel as in the English "baby." Hence the Japanese pronunciation of the city "Tōkyō" is "toh[held for two syllables]-kyoh [held for two syllables]," not the "toh-kee-yoh" one often hears in Anglicized pronunciation.

"f" is somewhere between an English "f" and "h" (like saying the English "f" sound without biting the lower lip).

"n" is like the English consonant and not to be confused with the "n'" nasalizer following a vowel. It never occurs at the end of a syllable because all syllables end in vowel sounds.

"r" is a difficult sound for English speakers (just as the English "r" is for Japanese speakers). As an approximation, imagine a British person saying "very good" so that it almost sounds like "veddy good." Sounding a little like a soft "d," it is made in the mouth quite differently—the tongue rolls forward over the palate instead of snapping against the front teeth.

Further Reading

Because this book is an introductory survey, it is subject to generalizations that would benefit from elaboration or qualification. Fortunately, there are fine resources available to interested readers. This is a short list of relevant works by major scholars that can be used to follow up themes introduced in this book. Most also contain good bibliographies that would guide the reader further still.

Two classic studies influential in Western scholarship on Shinto:
> Holtom, D. C. *The National Faith of Japan.* New York: Dutton, 1938.
> Hori, Ichiro. *Folk Religion in Japan: Continuity and Change.* Edited by Joseph M. Kitagawa and Alan L. Miller. Chicago: University of Chicago Press, 1968.

Translations of the ancient chronicles:
> Aston, W. G., trans. *Nihongi: Chronicles of Japan from the Earliest Times to A.D. 687.* London: Allen & Unwin, 1956. Originally published in 1896.
> Philippi, Daniel L., trans. *Kojiki.* Princeton: Princeton University Press, 1969.

Encyclopedic guides to terms, sites, persons, and other things related to Shinto:
> Bocking, Brian. *A Popular Dictionary of Shinto.* Surrey: Curzon Press, 1996.
> Picken, Stuart D. B. *Essentials of Shinto: An Analytical Guide to Principal Teachings.* Westport, Conn.: Greenwood Press, 1994.

Anthropological studies of Shinto in everyday life of Japanese with emphasis on particular sites:
> Nelson, John K. *A Year in the Life of a Shinto Shrine.* Seattle: University of Washington Press, 1996.
> ———. *Enduring Identities: The Guise of Shinto in Contemporary Japan.* Honolulu: University of Hawai'i Press, 2000.

Historical, anthropological study of the design and purpose of the ancient Kasuga shrine and its rituals:

Grapard, Allan G. *The Protocol of the Gods: A Study of the Kasuga Cult in Japanese History*. Berkeley: University of California Press, 1992.

Balanced, well-documented study of Shinto and institutionalization of state ideology:

Hardacre, Helen. *Shinto and the State: 1868–1988*. Princeton: Princeton University Press, 1989.

Two works on the Native Studies movement, the first emphasizing political ideologies, the second literary aspects:

Harootunian, Harry D. *Things Seen and Unseen: Discourse and Ideology in Tokugawa Nativism*. Chicago: University of Chicago Press, 1988.

Nosco, Peter. *Remembering Paradise: Nativism and Nostalgia in Eighteenth-Century Japan*. Cambridge, Mass.: Council on East Asian Studies, Harvard University; distributed through Harvard University Press, 1990.

Outstanding anthology of essays by experts on different historical periods in Shinto development:

Breen, John, and Mark Teeuwen, eds. *Shinto in History: Ways of the Kami*. Honolulu: University of Hawai'i Press, 2000.

On the role of women in Shinto:

Yusa, Michiko. "Women in Shinto: Images Remembered." In Arvind Sharma, ed., *Religion and Women*. Albany: SUNY Press, 1994.

A fine overview of Japanese religion today including some excellent information about Shinto:

Reader, Ian. *Religion in Contemporary Japan*. Honolulu: University of Hawai'i Press, 1991.

For further explanation of the relation between philosophical models and cultural difference (internal vs. external relations, holograph vs. whole-as-parts paradigms, personal vs. public knowledge):

Kasulis, Thomas P. *Intimacy or Integrity: Philosophy and Cultural Difference*. Honolulu: University of Hawai'i Press, 2002.

Index

English terms in parentheses are not translations or exact equivalences of the Japanese terms preceding them. They are only general definitions. Boldface page numbers indicate where Japanese terms are more fully defined in the text.

Dimensions of Asian Spirituality

Shinto: The Way Home
Thomas P. Kasulis

Chan Buddhism
Peter D. Hershock